The Party Line

Sheryl Longin & Roger L. Simon

Introduction by Ronald Radosh

The Party Line

A Play in Two Acts

CRITERION BOOKS

NEW YORK

First American edition published in 2012 by Criterion Books,
an activity of the Foundation for Cultural Review, Inc.,
a nonprofit, tax exempt corporation.
Criterion Books website: *www.newcriterion.com/books*

Manufactured in the United States and printed on acid-free paper.
The paper used in this publication meets the minimum requirements of
ANSI/NISO Z39.48–1992 (R 1997) (*Permanence of Paper*).

FIRST AMERICAN EDITION

LIBRARY OF CONGRESS CATALOGING-IN-PUBLICATION DATA

Longin, Sheryl, 1964–
The party line : a full-length play / Sheryl Longin & Roger L. Simon ;
introduction by Ronald Radosh.
   p.   cm.
Includes bibliographical references and index.
ISBN 978-0-9859052-0-0 (pbk. : alk. paper)
1. Duranty, Walter, 1884–1957—Drama. 2. Communism—Drama.
I. Simon, Roger Lichtenberg, 1943–. II. Radosh, Ronald. III. Title.
PS3612.O534P37 2012
812'.6—dc23
2012034343

CONTENTS

INTRODUCTION

SHERYL LONGIN and Roger L. Simon have accomplished a breathtaking feat in their imaginative and topical play, *The Party Line*. The title, as students of Communism know, refers to one's adherence to the current position on an issue as outlined by the Communist Party in its heyday. In those pristine days from the 1920s through the late 1940s and into the period of the early Cold War, it was necessary to check back each week to learn the "correct" position on any given issue, since the Party line would inexorably change as the winds blowing from Moscow forced the comrades to reconsider their earlier views.

The clearest example of this recurring process was the signing of the Nazi-Soviet Pact on August 23, 1939, that lasted until the German invasion of Soviet Russia on June 22, 1941. Overnight, the anti-fascist Communist parties of the world, under instructions from the Kremlin, dropped their anti-fascism, portrayed Adolf Hitler as a benign leader of a peaceful power, and sought to describe the Western leaders, Winston Churchill and Franklin D. Roosevelt, as fascists and war makers. After the invasion, orders came from Moscow to call for Western unity and a unified front with the West to defeat fascism.

The Longin–Simon play is set in both the Moscow of the early 1930s and the present-day Europe and United States. It centers on the antics, life, and career of the noted *New York Times* correspondent in Moscow, Walter Duranty. Moving from the past to the present day, the playwrights present Duranty's son – about whose real whereabouts and life we know virtually nothing – as a gay man living in Europe, where his lover is the soon to be assassinated Dutch political leader, Pim Fortuyn.

In both time periods, the authors present compromised journalists; from our own time, one from CNN; from the past, a man they name Harold Denny, a journalist groomed by Duranty to follow in his footsteps, misreporting the truth about the Soviet revolution to gullible American readers. He is contrasted with Denny's opposite, a man named Sid Brody, whose commitment to the truth leads him to eventually break ranks, thereby ending his standing on Soviet Press Commissar Konstantin Oumansky's list of approved journalists. In doing so, he also gives up any chance of achieving the high regard held for Duranty by the American establishment, who prefers the lies as long as it allows the Roosevelt administration to move along with its decision to give diplomatic recognition to Stalin's regime, ending the policy of non-recognition that had been in effect since Woodrow Wilson's presidency.

There was, of course, a very real Walter Duranty. Ask any journalist to name the most disreputable figure in their profession, and one name immediately comes to mind—the late *New York Times* reporter, Walter Duranty. Duranty is most well-known for his reportage of the Ukrainian famine created by Joseph Stalin in the early 1930s, where he covered up the deaths of hundreds of thousands of peasants as a fantasy and then perversely ran false reports written from Moscow about the success of Soviet agricultural policy. More dismaying is that his reporting from Moscow won him the very first Pulitzer Prize given to *The New York Times* for its foreign coverage in 1932.

The announcement of the prize given Duranty proclaimed that "Mr. Duranty's dispatches show profound and intimate comprehension of conditions in Russia and of the causes of those conditions. They are marked by scholarship, profundity, impartiality, sound judgement, and exceptional clarity, and are excellent examples of the best type of foreign correspondence." Reading those words today makes one think that either the Pulitzer Prize committee of its day was willfully blind or perhaps just stupid, given that everything Duranty wrote was in reality the opposite of the features they singled out for praise.

Let us skip ahead to the 1970s when the world learned, at first from the scholar Robert Conquest, about the reality of the starvation and decimation of the Ukranian people as a result of Stalin's Five Year Plan, and later from others who verified Conquest's work and deepened our knowledge. Each year when the Times listed the Pulitizers earned for that year, one couldn't help noticing Duranty's name at the top of the list as if the paper's publishers remained proud of his discredited coverage.

As the *Times* was subjected to increasing pressure to do something about this travesty, it decided to establish a blue ribbon commission that would investigate and report on the question of whether or not the paper should remove Duranty's name from the list, and, in effect, hand back the 1932 Pulitzer to the Pulitzer Board. Had they done that, it would mean that the paper's publisher fully acknowledged the fraudulent nature of the thirteen articles and two magazine stories for which Duranty was given the most coveted prize in journalism.

The paper asked Columbia University Professor of Russian History, Mark von Hagen, to review Duranty's work. Professor von Hagen concluded that Duranty "frequently writes in the enthusiastically propagandistic language of his sources," and that there was "a serious lack of balance in his writing." A good deal "of the 'factual' material," he wrote in his study of Duranty's dispatches, "is dull and largely uncritical recitation of Soviet sources, whereas his efforts at 'analysis' are very effective renditions of the Stalinist leadership's self-understanding of their murderous and progressive project to defeat the backwardness of Slavic, Asiatic peasant Russia."

Turning to the main reason why he thought that *The*

Times should turn down the award, von Hagen wrote that the "lack of balance and uncritical acceptance of the Soviet self-justification for its cruel and wasteful regime was a disservice to the American readers of *The New York Times* and the liberal values they subscribe to and to the historical experience of the peoples of the Russian and Soviet empires and their struggle for a better life." In an interview with the paper after he handed in his report, von Hagen added that the paper's publisher should "take it away for the greater honor and glory of *The New York Times*," since Duranty was a "disgrace" in the paper's history.

The editors, having asked von Hagen to make a report, acknowledged its validity in a signed editorial by a member of its editorial Board in 1990. Board member Karl E. Meyer called Duranty's work "some of the worst reporting to appear in this newspaper." Yet the paper's editor and publisher still refused to tell the Pulitzer committee it was handing back the award. The Executive Editor at the time, Bill Keller, agreed that "the work Duranty did ... was credulous, uncritical parroting of propaganda." Yet, Keller asserted that as a reporter who covered the Soviet Union for the paper in the late 1980s to 1991, "the notion of airbrushing history kind of gives me the creeps."

Keller's rationale makes no sense whatsoever. Stalinist airbrushing of purged Soviet leaders who were once highly regarded is hardly comparable to handing back a Pulitzer for reports that stay in the archives of the *Times*, and that are accessible to anyone. In no way were his dispatches airbrushed from history. And in no way did the paper's official statement make sense. The paper's publisher agreed that all of Duranty's work was false, and was completely "discredited." He noted that, had Duranty spoken to "ordinary Russians," he would have found out the truth at the time. Moreover, the publisher wrote that to examine what Russians thought, Duranty quoted "not a single one–only Stalin." Yet, they passed the buck to the Pulitzer Board, noting that they too had not rescinded the award. If the Pulitzer Board did not find it embarrassing, why, then, should the *Times*? Finally, the publisher invoked a meaningless and the most mundane excuse: "*The Times*," the publisher wrote, "does not have the award in its possession."

Like the newspaper, the Pulitzer Board also commissioned their own study of Duranty's work. For some reason, it took them six full months to investigate the issue, and on November 21, 2003, they announced that they would not revoke the prize it gave Duranty in 1932. The Board's logic says a great deal about how it functions. First, it acknowledged that "by today's standards for foreign reporting," Duranty's work "falls seriously short." Noting that in particular his future reports on the Ukranian famine of 1932–33 "have been criticized as gravely defective," they went on to argue that "a Pulitzer Prize for reporting is awarded not for the author's body of work or for the author's character but for the specific pieces entered in the competition." The Board said it focused only precisely on the thirteen articles handed to them by the paper, and finding no problem with the entries, concluded that the award would stand.

Most egregious was the Pulitzer Board's statement, easily disproved, that "there was not clear and convincing evidence of deliberate deception, the relevant standard in this case." That, of course, was patently untrue, since even when Duranty was alive, Malcolm Muggeridge, for one, had written in his dispatches that millions had died in the Ukraine. So did the British journalist Gareth Jones. As correspondent in Russia for the *Manchester Guardian*, and once a fellow traveler himself, Muggeridge later wrote the following about Duranty.

There was something vigorous, vivacious, preposterous, about his unscrupulousness which made his persistent lying somehow absorbing. I suppose no one ... followed the Party line, every shift and change, as assiduously as he did. In [the Soviet censor's] eyes he was perfect, and was constantly held up to the rest of us as an example of what we should be.

Gareth Jones even protested at the time Duranty wrote his dispatches, and had the *Times* looked in its own archives, they would have found his letter to the editor directly challenging Duranty's reporting. In a letter published on May 13th, 1933, Jones wrote that he visited many Russian villages, and "heard the cry, 'There is no bread, we are dying,' and that there was famine in the Soviet Union, menacing the lives of millions of people." Duranty then "cabled a denial of the famine" and replied that Jones' judgement was based on a forty-mile "tramp through villages." He too, Duranty wrote, had asked Soviet leaders and had come to the conclusion that there was no famine, and only food shortages.

Jones had in fact made three different visits to Soviet Russia, had traveled to twenty villages in both the Ukraine and black earth district, and outer Moscow as well. He too spoke to consuls and foreign representatives, all of whom backed up his reports. In response to Duranty's protests of his dispatches, Jones noted that journalists had to deal with censors, and hence "they give 'famine' the polite name of 'food shortage' and 'starving to death' is softened down to read as 'widespread mortality from diseases due to malnutrition.'"

At the same time Duranty was reporting from Moscow, the work of courageous and truthful journalists like Gareth Jones and Malcolm Muggeridge gives the lie to those who argue that the Pulitzer could not be returned, because the standards of the day were different.

Duranty's dishonest reporting was evident from the start, in the years before the Ukraine famine. It can be seen as well in his coverage of the Stalin show trials in 1936 and 1937. Of course, he was not alone in telling gullible western readers that the trials had proved the guilt of all those accused by the Stalinist machinery of state. That job was carried out by the U.S. Ambassador to the Soviet Union, Joseph Davies, whose best-selling 1941 book, *Mission to Moscow*, informed the American public that Stalin had destroyed very real conspiracies hatched against him by the Bolshevik's founding fathers.

The ignorance of Davies, of course, does not excuse Duranty's own gullibility. For example, on January 24, 1937, Duranty watched Georgi Pyatakov, one of the accused, testify. Pyatakov may have "looked like a professor," he wrote, but "what he told was a tale of black treason in act and intent." His testimony was not that of a "hysterical confession of a despairing fanatic, but a detailed recital of conspirative action ... more convincing than the indictment."

In a later dispatch, on February 14, 1937, Duranty reported that "Trotskyists abroad" were attacking the Soviet regime but had "drawn a red herring across the trial in the form of a story about a 'new and ruthless purge of the Communist party from top to bottom.'" Duranty explained to *Times'* readers that the purges simply meant "cleansing ... a milder word" that had "occurred periodically in the Communist party since the earliest days." It was simply a matter of Party members having their "Fitness" judged to see if they were worthy of being Communists. Nevertheless, Duranty noted that "it is obvious and reasonable to suppose that a minute investigation is being conducted of former oppositionists, especially Trotskyists." As he explained, "When men so high placed as Pyatakov, Radek, Sokolnikoff, and Lifshitz are sentenced as traitors it is only nature that other former oppositionists fall under suspicion." True to form, Duranty told readers that "The majority of persons now being investigated will probably get a clean bill of health" since the "Trotskyists' conspiracy" is made up of "numerically few."

In yet another dispatch by Duranty on the second round of the purge trials, Duranty complained in a January 30, 1937 dispatch that it was a shame "that no documentary evidence was produced in open court" that verified the espionage conducted by "men in such high positions" that the prosecutors claimed had taken place. Yet, he assured readers that "the trial did 'stand up' and should go far" to reveal the truth that "Trotsky is now revealed before the workers of the Union of Soviet Socialist Republics and the rest of the world as an ally of fascism and of a preparer of war and therefore, definitely finished as a force of international importance." Duranty also supported the death sentence handed down to men like Pyatakov, since, as he wrote, "There is no middle choice ... He knowingly organized a counter revolutionary group" that attempted sabotage and murder, which he told readers "is an unpardonable sin." It evidently did not occur to Duranty that the Soviet regime produced no documentary evidence for the would-be treason, since they had none.

What, one must ask, led a reporter like Duranty to engage in such blatant propaganda for the Stalinist regime, and to offer his observations on its behalf to American readers as truth? Duranty went so far as to praise the GPU – the new name given the CHEKA – as a body that did not torture and which was committed to the truth. The reason men confessed was not that they were tortured, but only because Russians had been given "sufficient proof" at the trials of the defendant's crimes. The forced confessions were simply a Russian "unburdening of the soul" similar to the confession made by individuals in the Catholic Church.

In a major *Times Magazine* article, Duranty sought to

explain what lay behind the conflict between Leon Trotsky and Joseph Stalin. Appearing on February 7th, 1937, it might have been written by Stalin's own loyal henchmen and appeared in the pages of *Pravda* or *Izvestia* (reminding one of the old Soviet joke: "There's no truth in *Pravda* and no news in *Izvestia*.) After Lenin died, Duranty explained, Stalin listened to the masses, while Trotsky engaged in "intrigue and conspirative cabals." He was not surprised, Duranty wrote, since Trotsky had started as a Menshevik rather than a Bolshevik, who always had attacked Lenin's major ideas, while Stalin supported them.

The above explanation, as any reader of scores of biographies of Trotsky knows well, is not only completely false, but simply parrots the official Stalinist explanation of the conflict almost verbatim. He went on to explain:

> Trotsky's mainspring was personal ambition, whereas Stalin was 'Lenin's disciple and a prolonger of Lenin's work,' as he told me himself on Christmas Day of 1933. In other words, Stalin from the outset was true to the Bolshveiks' ideology, whereas Trotsky from the outset to his present lamentable position was a Trotskyist first, last, and always.

Any of the myriad examples one can draw from Duranty's reporting fully justifies the title his biographer S. J. Taylor gave Duranty for the book she wrote, *Stalin's Apologist: Walter Duranty: The New York Times's Man in Moscow*. As hard as this is to digest, we learn from Taylor of Duranty's membership in a sadistic cult led by one Aleister Crowley, who called himself "the Beast," or "Beast 666," the anti-Christ predicted in the Book of Revelation. Claiming to be a dark magician, he arrived in Paris to practice black arts and magic-sexual rituals, which soon captivated the young Duranty, living in Paris in the days before the First World War. Here, with Crowley, Duranty partook of opium while engaging in sexual acts with as many women as he could muster to his side.

His foray into journalism began with the First World War, during which he covered the Belgian front. At the war's end, he reported on the Paris Peace Conference. Sent to the Balkans, Duranty was appointed Moscow correspondent of the *Times* in 1921. In Moscow, Duranty would quickly learn that the way to prosper and get notoriety was to ingratiate himself with Moscow's rulers. He traveled in an American Buick imported from the US that was driven by a Soviet chauffeur. In addition, the delighted Kremlin rulers saw to it that at a time of horrendous deprivation, he was given his own rather luxurious apartment, where he lived with his mistress and their child. By Western standards, it was not much, but as Taylor writes, "in Moscow in those days it was unwonted luxury." When regular Russians had to share apartments with multiple families, Duranty had his own that included a separate bedroom, dining room, and private office, as well as his personal telephone.

When he returned to the United States in 1933 – after the false famine reports had appeared and he had won his Pulitzer, FDR welcomed him to the White House, in a move meant to provide backing for the President's desire to have the US recognize the Soviet Union and develop formal diplomatic relations with the USSR. Duranty was the star at the official dinner for the amiable first Soviet Ambassador to the US, Maxim Litvinov. "At last," Taylor puts it, "he was reaping his reward." 1500 major industrial and political leaders dined at the Waldorf-Astoria in New York City in support of recognition of the Soviets. But it was only the introduction of Duranty to the assembled prestigious audience that got the body to its feet, as they rose from their chairs and cheered.

Returning to Moscow, Duranty was summoned to the Kremlin by none other than Stalin himself, who gave him an exclusive interview on Christmas day of 1933. Stalin told him:

> You have done a good job in your reporting the U.S.S.R., though you are not a Marxist, because you try to tell the truth about our country and to understand it and explain it to your readers. I might say you bet on our horse to win when others thought it had no chance and I am sure you have not lost by it.

Duranty may have won the war as best foreign correspondent, but the praise heaped upon him by the Soviet tyrant in our own day is the single most damning indictment of his reporting. Stalin's unasked tribute to Duranty – if indeed Stalin actually said those words or Duranty made them up himself – paint the *Times'* man in Moscow to have been nothing but a propagandist – doing the Kremlin's job in America better than any of its own paid agents could have.

How fitting that *The New Criterion* is announcing its first annual Walter Duranty Award, to be given for the worst news story in an American newspaper or magazine in the previous year. Some of those nominated might indeed be considered deans of American journalism, much as Duranty was considered in his own day. Our board will be scrupulous and fair-minded in making its choice, and will select a prize winner whose journalism can compare to that of Walter Duranty. Unfortunately, in these times, there will most likely be many candidates for the "honor," and hence the task may not be too hard to accomplish.

RONALD RADOSH

The Party Line

CAST OF CHARACTERS

(in order of appearance – to be performed by a company of seven – see note below)

3

ALEISTER CROWLEY – *Early 20th-century British occultist*

PREGNANT WIVES – *there are two*

WALTER DURANTY – *Moscow correspondent for* The New York Times

JANE CHARON – *Duranty's first wife*

MICHAEL DURANTY – *Walter Duranty's son*

STOCKTON RHODES – *a CNN journalist*

SID BRODY – *Moscow correspondent for UPI*

ROSE BRODY – *Sid's wife*

MARK KRAVITZ – *a New York theater director*

KONSTANTIN OUMANSKY – *director of the Soviet Press Office*

KATYA – *Walter Duranty's Russian "wife"*

HAROLD DENNY – *a young reporter in Moscow*

COMRADE ZAVANOVA – *Moscow peasant woman*

FIRS – *Zavanova's cousin from the Ukraine*

PIM FORTUYN – *a Dutch politician*

DIANA PIERSON – *an American heiress*

CONSTANCE BUSHNELL – *Diana's friend*

CECIL B. DEMILLE – *a movie mogul*

FRANCES – *Walter Duranty's lady friend in Florida*

4   The actors' roles are intended to be doubled in the following manner:

Walter Duranty / Michael Duranty

Sid Brody / Pim Fortuyn

Diana Pierson / Comrade Zavanova / Pregnant Wife

Katya / Constance Bushnell / Pregnant Wife

Stockton Rhodes / Konstantin Oumansky / Aleister Crowley

Mark Kravitz / Harold Denny / Firs / Cecil B. DeMille

Rose Brody / Jane Charon / Frances

ACT ONE

From a darkened stage comes the sound of voices chant-ing. The words are indistinguishable but it's some sort of religious liturgy. Suddenly a man's voice rings out clearly.

MAN'S VOICE (CROWLEY) *(with British accent)*

Let the magician, robed and armed as he may deem to be fit, turn to face towards Boleskine, that is the House of the Beast 666.

LIGHTS SLOWLY FADE UP ON –

A group of worshippers.

Standing in front of a statue of Horus and next to an urn on a pedestal is their leader – a man wearing a cloak and a large pyramid for a hat. This is the famous bohemian and Satanist, ALEISTER CROWLEY. He is flanked by his two PREGNANT WIVES, also in robes. Standing in front of him, also in robes, are a man in his thirties – WALTER DURANTY – and his wife, JANE.

Strike the battery 1 – 3 – 3 – 3 – 1.

The wives strike drums.

(to Duranty)

Put the thumb of your right hand between its index and medius and make the gestures hereafter following.

DURANTY *(also with British accent)*

Sweet Jesus, Crowley. Sometimes your stuff can be a tad cornball for a Satanist.

6

CROWLEY

You joined the club. Now live with it... Besides, this is your celebration.

Duranty makes a face, but complies, adjusting his thumb accordingly. Crowley places his hands on Duranty's and Jane's shoulders.

(incanting)

Here on the banks of the Hudson River, in the year of somebody's lord – 1920 – I, Aleister Crowley, put the Mark of the Beast on that devoted follower of our order, Walter Duranty, and his wife Jane, in honor of Walter's glorious new appointment to bring forth our wisdom from the Russian lands... May his Sexual Magick thrive as has mine before him...

Crowley pats the pregnant stomachs of his wives. Then he ignites a torch.

CROWLEY

Let the Magician clasp his hands upon his wand, his fingers and thumbs interlaced, crying, "LASHTAL! THELEMA! FIAOF! AGAPE! AUMGN"!

DURANTY *(tongue half in cheek)*

Does this mean we can take off our clothes now?

CROWLEY

According to the precepts of our order... Do what you will!

He starts to ignite the urn.

But first, inhale the holy ether and coca!

The ether mixed with cocaine starts to smoke as they all inhale and start stripping off their clothes for an orgy.

LIGHTS OUT.

SCENE TWO

LIGHTS UP ON –

MICHAEL'S Amsterdam apartment. May 2002.

An elegant, minimalist living room where MICHAEL DURANTY, a handsome man of a certain age, is seated on a pale leather sofa. A doorbell rings. He sighs, gets up. Slowly walks to the front door and opens it.

MICHAEL *(with a slight Russian accent)*

I was wondering if or when you would show up. Come in, my friend.

Through the door steps a significantly younger American man, STOCKTON RHODES. He is slight and boyish, although obviously in his forties. He moves forward awkwardly, half extending his hand at the same time as leaning forward to embrace Michael, who does neither, instead delicately stepping aside, smiling at Stockton.

STOCKTON *(concerned)*

How are you holding up, Michael?

MICHAEL

I always told Pim the stress of being with him all these years would kill me.

(he smiles)

As usual, he had the last laugh.

STOCKTON

The Dutch seem genuinely devastated. Like a hero has been felled.

MICHAEL

Because that is the fact. He was the most popular candidate for Prime Minister of this country in next week's election. Somehow, I imagine the rest of the world and your very important American media will paint it otherwise, as usual. Which is why you are here.

He goes to a bejeweled and gilded Russian samovar con- spicuously displayed on an otherwise unadorned sidebar.

Would you like a cup?

STOCKTON *(admiring it)*

Who could say no to that? It's fantastic.

MICHAEL

Pim called it the poisoned well. Drink from it at your own risk. He always refused.

STOCKTON

Because it belonged to your father?

Michael shrugs.

The unrepentant, in your face atheist, Pim Fortuyn, indulged in silly superstition? That's a surprise.

MICHAEL

Not at all if you understand who he is . . . was.

He quickly starts making tea in the samovar checking his emotions.

Are you going to use that in your reporting? A personal detail that no one but the intrepid Stockton Rhodes of CNN managed to unearth?

He hands Stockton a cup of tea.

STOCKTON

Everything's off the record, Michael, unless you're okay with it.

MICHAEL

I'm not okay with any of this and I never will be. Don't try to make yourself feel better by getting my permission. It doesn't matter. No one will tell the truth anyway.

LIGHTS OUT.

SCENE THREE

LIGHTS UP ON –

The interior of an ocean liner. Day.

It's 1928 and that date is projected onto the scrim. We're in a tiny third-class cabin, which is just suggested by a couple of walls and a porthole. ROSE and SID BRODY – a young idealistic couple of the period – are saying goodbye to their close friend MARK KRAVITZ. The Brody's baby, Emma, is in a bassinet next to a narrow double-decker bed.

MARK

I'm so jealous.

BRODY

Of what? Eight days in the lowest deck of third class in a room not even big enough for a goldfish?

MARK

Who needs a goldfish? You've got Emma and Rose. The three of you are headed to make history and you've left me behind... Plus, you've got a porthole all your own.

ROSE

That you have to stand on tiptoe to see out of.

MARK

Grumble, grumble, grumble... They don't even have Prohibition over there. I'd cut off my right hand to go with you.

   (to Brody)

Do you realize what this does for you? You'll be a hero of the working class. They'll make you editor of the Daily Worker, maybe the New York Times.

BRODY

They've already got Walter Duranty. Who could fill his shoes?

MARK

Ah, yes... the great Duranty... Then Minister of Culture!

BRODY

In that case, I'd make you Director of the People's Theatre.

MARK

With pleasure, amigo. And find me a wife while you're at it.

There's a loud blast from the ship's smokestack.

One of those statuesque types from the socialist-realist movies.

ROSE

Rosy-cheeked with pigtails, driving a tractor.

MARK

Tractors are sexy.

The smokestack blows again.

Oops, I guess that's bye-bye. I love you guys.

(wraps his arms around both of them) (leans over the bassinet)

Emma, we want you to grow up in a socialist America. Your parents didn't name you after Emma Goldman for nothing. Desvadanya, tovarich.

He blows the baby a kiss and starts off.

LIGHTS OUT.

SCENE FOUR

LIGHTS UP ON –

An austere Soviet office.

We are in the Press Department of the People's Commissariat of Foreign Affairs, Moscow. Press Chief KONSTANTIN OUMANSKY sits opposite Brody and Rose who tends to baby Emma sleeping in the bassinet. On the scrim in an old typewriter font: "Moscow – May 17, 1928: Communist Party General Secretary Joseph Stalin announced a formal Five Year Plan today for the Soviet Union, effectively ending the limited capitalism of Vladimir Lenin's New Economic Policy."

OUMANSKY

So you have some problems with your new apartment, Mr. and Mrs. Brody?

BRODY

No, no. It's ... quite spacious.

ROSE

We can see the Moscow River from the bathroom window.

OUMANSKY

Shared bathroom... Not perhaps what you were used to in New York.

BRODY *(making light)*

We lived in a tiny one-bedroom on Essex. Just above the TASS office.

OUMANSKY

Yes. Where you worked for four years, before getting this assignment. My congratulations to you and your wife. The United Press is what you Americans call a big deal, is it not? And clever of them to choose you, I might add.

ROSE

They picked the next John Reed.

BRODY

Rose, please...

OUMANSKY

"Ten Days That Shook the World, Part II," by Sid Brody. It has a certain ring to it.

    (to Rose)

Are you Louise Bryant?

    Just then the baby starts to cry. Rose goes to comfort her.

ROSE *(suddenly courageous)*

What we really need is a refrigerator.

OUMANSKY

But of course. For the baby's milk. We will look into it right away.

ROSE

Only if it's not putting anyone out. We realize there are more pressing matters here.

    Oumansky takes out a stamp and paper from the desk.

OUMANSKY

Mr. Brody, your first article...

    He stamps it.

Approved by the People's Commissariat of Foreign Affairs.

    He passes it to Brody who seems pleased.

                          LIGHTS OUT.

SCENE FIVE

> *LIGHTS UP ON –*

14

> *The Metropole Hotel Bar. Night.*

> *A decaying remnant of the Czarist era, the bar of the Metropole is the hangout for bohemians and others in the Soviet Union of the twenties and thirties. A painted backdrop shows other tables filled with people. We hear lots of chatter in English. At a table in the dead center of the room sits Walter Duranty – now fortysomething – with a younger American journalist, HAROLD DENNY, and a very pretty Russian girl, KATYA. Oumansky enters the bar and heads toward Duranty's table.*

DENNY *(to Duranty)*

How did you manage to get a car and driver, Walter? I don't even have running water in my room.

> *Duranty smiles, lights the first of a never-ending stream of cigarettes.*

DURANTY

When the vodka is of this standard and dirt cheap, why on earth would you ever need water? Right, Comrade Oumansky?

> *Oumansky smiles and takes a seat at the table.*

OUMANSKY *(to Denny)*

The Dictatorship of the Proletariat respects Comrade Duranty's astute observation of our progress in modernization and his articles allow the world to see us as we truly are. So when we learned that he had suffered the loss of a leg in an unfortunate accident. . .

> *Duranty hops up, rolling up his trouser to reveal a wooden leg underneath.*

DURANTY

From each according to his ability, to each according to his need.

> *He gestures to Katya, seated beside Denny. She is staring, fascinated, at his wooden leg.*

DURANTY

Come over here. Give it a knock. It's good luck.

> *To Denny's astonishment, without hesitating, the girl gets up and goes over to Duranty and raps on the exposed false limb.*

What's your name? You're exceptionally pretty.

> *The girl smiles, suddenly a little shy.*

KATYA *(with a thick Russian accent)*

Katya.

DURANTY

Yes, Katya, it's just like rubbing the Buddha's belly, very good luck indeed. How would you like to be the personal assistant to the New York Times Moscow correspondent? It's a twenty-four-hour-a-day job, but you're young and healthy looking. Up to the task, I'm sure.

> *Oumansky is watching, amused, as Denny grows increasingly upset.*

And the benefits are quite excellent.

He winks at her and hands her a blini piled with caviar. She grabs it and devours it in one bite.

DENNY

But she's my translator! It took me weeks to find a decent one!

Katya looks nervously at Oumansky, unsure what to do. Oumansky nods to her to stay with Duranty.

OUMANSKY *(to Denny)*

You need just have asked in the first place. I'll have another translator sent to you in the morning.

Denny gets up from the table in a huff.

DENNY

I've only been here three months but I was hoping to preserve my delusion of a free press for just a little longer.

He looks over at Duranty, who has his arm around Katya, then turns and walks out, passing Sid and Rose Brody, who are just entering the bar. They both recognize him and smile.

BRODY

Harold! You still with the Chicago Trib? I didn't know they had a correspondent in Moscow.

DENNY

They won't for much longer. Really, there's no need for anyone to be here with the great Walter Duranty covering the scene.

ROSE

Is he here tonight? We've heard about him constantly since we arrived, but haven't met him yet.

> *Denny points to the table where Duranty sits with Katya on his lap.*

DENNY

You can take my seat, and my former translator's. She seems to have found a more comfortable one.

> *He walks out. Sid and Rose exchange curious glances as they approach the table.*

ROSE *(to Brody)*

Are you going to ask Comrade Oumansky about getting an interview with Comrade Stalin?

> *Brody looks at her and laughs, puts his arm around her affectionately.*

ROSE

What's so funny, darling?

BRODY

Every time I start to feel horribly guilty about dragging you and our baby into such miserable living conditions, you amaze me with your equanimity. "Comrade" Oumansky, "Comrade" Stalin? You're better at this than I am.

> *(he kisses her on the tip of her nose)*

How'd I ever get so lucky?

ROSE *(winking at him)*

I liked your politics.

Oumansky sees them approaching.

OUMANSKY *(to Duranty)*

Your newest competition.

Duranty looks up curiously as Sid and Rose reach the table. Sid leans forward and extends his hand to Duranty.

BRODY

Sid Brody, United Press.

Duranty shakes it and then, removing Katya from his lap, stands with an air of British formality, and turns to Rose.

DURANTY

Mrs. Brody?

ROSE *(amused)*

Rose.

He genteelly takes her hand and kisses it.

DURANTY

Walter Duranty, the New York Times.

Oumansky gestures to the empty chairs.

OUMANSKY

Please, join us.

BRODY

We don't want to interrupt...

OUMANSKY

Nonsense. You've arrived at a most auspicious time. Comrade Duranty has just hired a new assistant.

Duranty pulls out a chair for Rose as Oumansky fills two fresh glasses with vodka and tops up the others. Rose and Brody sit down.

(raising his glass)

Na zdorovye.

Katya, having been ejected from Duranty's lap, stands awkwardly beside him as he sits back down, leaving no empty chairs. Duranty raises his glass towards Brody and Rose.

DURANTY

Welcome to the Soviet Union.

They all take a drink. Duranty casually pulls Katya back onto his lap.

LIGHTS OUT.

SCENE SIX

LIGHTS UP ON –

The Brodys' tiny flat. Night.

Brody is lying on the bed, struggling to read Pravda with the help of a dictionary while Rose roots about in their new refrigerator – a squat, noisy device of uncertain provenance. A few feet away, behind a curtain, the baby sleeps in the bassinet next to a rickety old couch.

BRODY *(to himself)*

Twelve thousand kolkhozy… Kolkhozy?

(checks dictionary)

Ah, collective farms...

(to Rose, re. fridge)

20   Is it working?

Before she can respond, there is a knock on the door. Brody goes to open it. COMRADE ZAVANOVA – a diminutive lady in a babushka – is standing there. Lurking behind her is a lanky, furtive man in threadbare clothes holding a tattered overnight bag – FIRS.

ZAVANOVA

Prezhalsta, Comrade Brody. I am sorry to disturb you and Mrs. Brody but my cousin had just arrived from Ukraine. We have no room in our bed with my sister's children and my cousin cannot sleep on the floor. He doesn't get enough to eat and has a bone disease.

Brody glances over at Rose who nods in acceptance.

BRODY

Well, he can use our couch, but I'm not sure it's all that soft.

Firs launches into a coughing fit.

ZAVANOVA

Don't worry. It is only from smoking. He will not infect the baby...

(ushering in the emaciated Firs)

That is very kind of you, Comrade. They say you are very sympathetic to us and they are right. Anyway, it will only be for one night. At most two. And Firs does not speak English. He will not disturb you.

ROSE

That's okay. Sid's learning Russian.

ZAVANOVA

That is good. Because Firs has an important story for you.

BRODY

He does?

ZAVANOVA

Yes. About Ukraine... where he comes from. A small village there. But not far from Kiev.

> *Zavanova looks around, makes sure the door is shut. Then...*

Some bad things are happening. No one will listen to him here. He heard you were a foreign journalist and wanted to tell you... So you can report it, Comrade Brody. For America.

> *Brody glances over at Rose who looks more than a little skeptical. He shrugs and turns back.*

BRODY

What is it, Comrade Zavanova?

> *She says something to Firs in Russian and the man starts to blurt out a story in a hoarse voice.*

> *(overwhelmed)*

Wait, wait, wait... My Russian is nowhere near that good yet...

> *(smiles)*

Three words... Desvedanya, prezhalsta and... kolkhozy.

ZAVANOVA *(frowns)*

Kolkhozy?

BRODY

Yes. Collective farm.

ZAVANOVA

I know.

BRODY *(gestures to couch)*

Sit. You can translate for him.

> *Firs begins to talk in Russian.*

> *LIGHTS FADE AS*

> *A series of gruesome black and white photographs appear on the scrim, showing peasants and children, animals as well, in extreme conditions of starvation. These are real photos of the Ukrainian "Holodomor" of 1932–33. In the dim light, while the photos display behind them, Zavanova and Brody continue their conversation.*

ZAVANOVA

So many people are starving in Ukraine. Thousands, he says. Maybe tens of thousands.

BRODY

Yes, I understand there has been a bad harvest.

ZAVANOVA

It is more than that. They are making the people starve. The Red Army does not allow the kulaks to have any grain from their own farms.

BRODY

The kulaks are capitalists. The government is trying to build socialism there. What else can they do but have them share the grain with everyone who needs it?

> *Firs speaks some more in Russian as the scrim shows photos of commissars loading corn and grain onto trains while starving peasants watch.*

ZAVANOVA

Firs says they steal all the kulaks' food and send it to Moscow. Then no one has anything to eat. Not the poor peasants or the kulaks, who aren't rich anymore anyway. Firs says this is all deliberate.

> *The scrim fades and the lights come up full in the apartment again.*

ROSE *(whispers to Zavanova)*

I hope Firs isn't a kulak.

ZAVANOVA *(shakes her head vehemently)*

He was a shoemaker – until he lost his fingers from frostbite. Poor Firs . . . first frostbite, then osteoporosis. What bad luck.

BRODY

I'm sorry to hear it.

> *(exhales, troubled)*

This is all hard to believe.

> *Zavanova translates once more for Firs who says something back in Russian.*

ZAVANOVA

He invites you to come to Ukraine and see the truth for yourself.

> *Brody hesitates, frowns.*

ROSE

You know you can't do that, Sid. The United Press restricts you to Moscow.

> *Brody looks torn when there is a sudden knock on the door. Everyone freezes. There is a second harder knock. Firs looks terrified and starts to shrink back against the wall. Brody goes and opens the door. Oumansky is standing there in full uniform. He steps brusquely into the flat and stops, surveying all the frozen faces. For a long moment, he says nothing. Then he turns to Brody.*

OUMANSKY

Congratulations, Comrade Brody. I have the pleasure of informing you that your request has been granted. You will be the first foreign correspondent with the privilege of a personal interview with our General Secretary Joseph Stalin.

> *Rose and Zavanova nearly gasp. Firs, having heard the name Stalin, looks questioningly at Zavanova. She explains in Russian. Firs, overwhelmed, sinks slowly down onto the bed.*

> *LIGHTS OUT.*

SCENE SEVEN

The sound of a typewriter fills the darkness.

LIGHTS UP ON –

DURANTY'S Moscow flat. Evening. Surprisingly spacious and well appointed, looking more like an apartment in Paris than one in the middle of the Communist capital of the world. Duranty is in a chair at a corner desk, typing rapidly. He hits the return button with a flourish and pushes himself away from the desk.

DURANTY

Another eight hundred scintillating words on the merits of agricultural collectivization. How do I do it?

(calling out)

Katya! Give us a kiss.

Katya enters from the kitchen, wearing an apron. She looks tired and a little pale. She hurries over to Duranty who pulls her onto his lap and kisses her.

You smell like onions.

He slips his hand under her skirt.

After my guests leave, you can translate my piece for the censors.

She nods. He kisses her again.

I'd like you with some caviar. Tell Comrade Oumansky I need copious amounts of the good stuff so I can eat it right off you.

She shakes her head, looking ashamed.

Shy? I don't think so. Never mind. I'll tell him myself.

There's a knock on the door. Katya leaps up, pulling down her skirt.

Is dinner almost ready?

She nods and heads back to the kitchen as Duranty gets up and opens the front door, revealing the younger journalist, Denny.

Entrez, dear boy. A drink or four await you chez Duranty.

He smiles magnanimously and ushers the uncomfortable looking Denny inside. Goes to the bar and fixes them drinks. Denny looks around, somewhat shocked by the cushy, bourgeois surroundings.

DENNY

Nice set up you've got here. I wouldn't let the locals see how the Great Duranty lives while they suffer or you'll trigger another revolution.

Duranty slaps him on the back and hands him a drink.

DURANTY

You're not still holding a grudge about that translator, are you? When you've been here as long as I have, and paid your dues, you'll have seniority... That's the grand Soviet way. Until then, drink up...

He takes a swig.

(calling out)

It makes the time go faster. Katya, where are the zakuski?

Katya re-enters, carrying a tray of hors d'œuvres. She sees Denny but betrays no reaction.

Tell me Katya, who takes better care of you? This handsome young whippersnapper or the old one legged scribbler?

KATYA

You do, Comrade Duranty.

DURANTY *(to Denny)*

See, it all worked out for the best. Stop being so selfish and think of the poor girl.

He smiles at Denny who doesn't return it.

Why still so glum, lad? Ah yes, I know. Same reason I've been down a bit myself . . . skipped right over by the damn Commissariat.

Katya, who is looking even paler and clammy, wipes her forehead with her apron and sinks down into a chair.

(oblivious to her)

How dare they grant the first interview with our man Stalin to someone fresh off the boat. It should have been mine. . . or at least, yours.

DENNY *(shakes his head)*

Sid Brody is a seasoned journalist. He's got the right credentials.

Duranty guffaws.

DURANTY

I'll say. Did you read that piece of agit prop he wrote? A Kremlin worshipping choir boy is what he is.

There's another knock at the door. Duranty goes to open it.

Propaganda is like treacle. A little bit goes a long way. Too much makes you swear off the stuff. And then what good is that?

> *He opens the door, all smiles again, to reveal Brody and Rose. Brody hands him a bottle of Russian vodka.*

ROSE *(apologetically)*

We tried desperately to find some British gin but. . .

DURANTY

Impossible. I've single-handedly polished off the last black market shipment.

> *He ushers them in, helping Rose off with her coat.*

Besides, we can't toast your husband's journalistic coup with anything other than champagne. Katya. . .

> *He points to the kitchen and Katya stands, looking weak, and exits in that direction.*

I've been saving a very special bottle for just this occasion. Of course, I have to admit I thought I'd be toasting myself.

> *Brody looks a little embarrassed.*

ROSE

It took us both by surprise too. I know Sid wasn't expecting that kind of access, especially so soon after we got here.

BRODY

I just sent a pro-forma request for an interview, same as every other foreign correspondent in every bureau of every paper around the world.

DENNY *(nods)*

I make a request to the Kremlin to interview Stalin practically every week. I think we all do.

DURANTY

Indeed. But for some reason, they saw fit to grant the very first one to you, Comrade Brody.

> *Katya re-enters carrying a tray with a bottle of champagne and glasses. She looks even paler, with beads of sweat on her upper lip.*

ROSE

Maybe it was a lottery. That would be the egalitarian Communist way.

> *Duranty chortles as he pops the cork and pours the first glass.*

DURANTY *(offering it to Rose)*

Ah, the bloom is still on Rose... Communism is practiced a bit differently on its home turf than within the democratic borders of New York City or Chicago.

BRODY

Are you suggesting I got the interview with Stalin for some ulterior reason?

> *Duranty shrugs.*
>
> *(defensively)*

I was caught off guard. I had less than an hour to prepare. Believe me, if I'm invited back, I've got a long list of questions to ask Stalin about his so-called workers' paradise.

ROSE

Nothing's perfect, Sid. But it's quite thrilling to be here. I'm inclined to agree with what Lincoln Steffens said after he visited: "I have seen the future and it works."

Just then, Katya starts to gag. She drops the tray and hurries out of the room. Everyone turns in her direction at the sounds of retching and vomiting.

ROSE *(concerned, calling out)*

Katya, are you alright? Do you need some help?

From off stage, the sound of Katya vomiting continues. Rose rushes off in her direction, exiting the stage. Denny looks at Duranty who is unfazed.

DURANTY

What? She hasn't been drinking. At least that I know of. If she had an alcohol problem when she was working for you, you might have told me.

Denny shakes his head.

BRODY *(realizing)*

Don't the Soviets have a law that says if you're living together, you're married?

Duranty makes a vague gesture.

DURANTY

I don't see what difference that makes.

LIGHTS OUT.

SCENE EIGHT

> *On the scrim flash the words:* AMSTERDAM, 1993

> *LIGHTS UP ON –*

> *The Galleria Gorbachev*

> *A small art gallery with its name painted in red Soviet-style calligraphy on a stark white wall. On exhibit are a collection of Russian antiquities of both Czarist and Soviet vintage. A spiral staircase leads up to a second level loft living quarters that is barely visible without illumination. On the ground level, a younger-looking Michael is setting up for an opening, putting out bottles of wine, plastic cups, etc. His back is to the entrance as the front bell rings and a man (PIM FORTUYN) enters – tall and charismatic, with a shaved head.*

FORTUYN *(with a Dutch accent)*

Am I too early for a glass of wine?

> *Michael turns around, startled.*

MICHAEL

The opening doesn't start for fifteen minutes.

> *He smiles and pours a glass of wine.*

But it's never too early for a drink.

> *He walks over to Fortuyn and hands him the cup.*

I don't think I've ever seen you here before.

FORTUYN

I've been walking past ever since it opened a few years ago, always meaning to stop in. Are you the owner?

Michael nods. Fortuyn looks around at the various pieces.

You have a magnificent eye.

He smiles at Michael.

I have what I've been told is an irritating habit of only going to museums and galleries when they open their doors so I can see the art without the distractions of a crowd. But I'm keeping you from getting ready for your party. My apologies.

MICHAEL *(smiles)*

You are most welcome. After all, I can't sell anything without patrons.

FORTUYN

True, but where are my manners? A stranger enters and doesn't even introduce himself... My name is Pim.

He extends his hand.

MICHAEL *(taking it)*

Michael.

They shake hands, holding on an extra beat. The attraction between them is palpable.

FORTUYN

You have a Russian accent. How long have you been living in the Netherlands?

MICHAEL

Since March 23, 1987 at 2:51 in the afternoon. But who's counting?

He pours himself a glass of wine and holds it up to Fortuyn's.

I propose a toast to my adopted home, the freest city in the world, Amsterdam.

FORTUYN

I couldn't agree more.

> *They clink glasses and share a flirtatious look.*

And I hope it stays this way.

> *They both take sips.*

MICHAEL

What is it that you do, Pim?

FORTUYN

I'm a recovering academic.

> *Michael looks at him curiously.*

A former Marxist professor of sociology.

> *(he grins)*

As an obviously successful capitalist yourself, please don't hold that against me. I'm undergoing a reformation.

MICHAEL

I'd like to hear about it. What's the catalyst for you change?

FORTUYN

I have a suspicion your story is more fascinating. May I call you sometime?

MICHAEL

I'm surprised to hear myself say this. It's quite out of character. But I think I'll be devastated if you don't.

The entry bell rings again, accompanied by the sounds of the first guests arriving.

Excuse me. Capitalism in action.

MICHAEL *(starting towards the front)*

My last name is Duranty. I'm in the phone book.

Hearing that name, Fortuyn looks surprised.

LIGHTS OUT.

The sounds of party-goers at the opening continues over the blackout, then gradually fades as. . .

LIGHTS UP ON –

The upstairs loft.

Late afternoon light spills in from a large open window at the back, illuminating Michael, bare-chested, propped up in bed beneath rumpled covers. Through the window, an Amsterdam street scape and storefront can be seen – the "Bordello Bambi 24/7" – with male and female mannequins dressed in bondage attire arranged in a provocative window display. Fortuyn appears at the top of the stairs from the darkened gallery below. He is carrying a tray with two bottles of beer and a bag of pretzels.

FORTUYN

Hope you don't mind that I ransacked your pantry. Since we skipped the lunch segment of our first date, I thought we might need something to tide us over until we have dinner.

MICHAEL *(smiles)*

"We" have dinner? How long is this first date going to last?

> *Fortuyn sets down the tray and tears open the bag of pretzels.*

FORTUYN

Until we get tired of each other, I suppose.

> *He pops a pretzel into Michael's mouth.*

MICHAEL

What if we don't?

FORTUYN

Hmmm. Hasn't happened to me before. That would be something.

MICHAEL

Never? Former Marxist professor Pim Fortuyn has never been in love?

FORTUYN *(climbing into bed)*

I never felt the compulsion. Lust is such an enjoyable diversion.

> *He kisses Michael on the mouth. It lasts a while. Through the window, a MUSLIM COUPLE can be seen walking past the bordello, the wife in full hijab. The husband tries to hustle her past, but she covertly sneaks a look at the mannequins, angering him. He grabs her roughly. In bed, Michael finally pulls back from the kiss.*

MICHAEL

They're not mutually exclusive.

FORTUYN

I'll never be monogamous, Michael.

Michael nods.

FORTUYN

36   Could you still love me anyway?

> *Through the window, the husband is visible slapping the woman hard across her face. She screams. Michael and Fortuyn hear the screams and jump out of bed. They run to the window and see what's happening on the street below.*

MICHAEL

I'll call the police.

FORTUYN

They won't do anything. They're afraid of being accused of racism.

> *He grabs his pants and starts pulling them on.*

MICHAEL

What are you going to do?

FORTUYN

Stop a man from beating a woman in broad daylight in the middle of a free country!

> *He runs down the stairs. Michael looks worried. He grabs his own clothes and follows.*

LIGHTS OUT.

SCENE NINE

Lights up on –

The Metropole Bar. Night.

Again, the stage is lit to make it appear crowded, with the sounds of American jazz and lots of patrons. But only the center table with Duranty, Brody and Rose is illuminated. Oumansky enters the bar, scowling, carrying a newspaper. He marches over to them and tosses the paper on the table.

OUMANSKY

These are capitalist lies! There is no famine. Some food shortages of course because of poor harvests in Ukraine this year. Not enough rain. But no one is starving.

Brody picks up the newspaper and reads aloud. As he does, the scrim is illuminated and the newspaper article is projected onto it. The headline reads: "FAMINE RULES RUSSIA: THE 5 YEAR PLAN HAS KILLED THE BREAD SUPPLY," BY GARETH JONES.

BRODY *(reading)*

"I walked along through villages... Everywhere was the cry, 'There is no bread. We are dying.' In the train a Communist denied to me that there was a famine. I flung a crust of bread which I had been eating from my own supply into a spittoon. A peasant fellow fished it out and ravenously ate it. I threw an orange peel into the spittoon and the peasant again grabbed it and devoured it.

Oumansky angrily swats the paper out of Brody's hands. He points to the byline.

OUMANSKY

I have never heard of this so called reporter who is obviously another Western agent. Just like the British engineers we are about to try for espionage. Who is he?

DURANTY *(leaning over to read the name)*

Of course, Gareth Jones.

   (smiling)

An energetic Welsh lad with the overzealous naiveté of youth.

OUMANSKY

The Dictatorship of the Proletariat is wearying of these pathetic efforts to cast international doubt on the great success of our Five Year Plan. You are all here at the gracious invitation of the Soviet Union and, as you well know, that invitation can be rescinded at any time.

DURANTY

My dear Oumansky, calm down. You can't possibly send our good friend Brody away. He and Rose just got here and are only just beginning to appreciate the extraordinary progress made since the revolution and the herculean effort that has been and continues to be required of every citizen.

OUMANSKY

Articles such as this jeopardize all that progress. This Gareth Jones is spitting in the face of the Soviet people who make enormous sacrifices to improve the lives of the workers of the world. It's up to you to refute his lies in the Western press.

BRODY

But what if he isn't lying? Peasants are starving in the Ukraine. Other countries can send food and supplies to remedy the shortage and alleviate the suffering. No one needs to die of starvation.

OUMANSKY

More help from the West? So you can infiltrate with more spies like the British engineers? We are quite capable of taking care of ourselves. Might I suggest you have a duty to your own countrymen to report on the trial of these Western agents, so that they learn of the crimes committed in their names by their own governments.

DURANTY

Perhaps the engineers are innocent, Comrade Oumansky.

OUMANSKY

The evidence will be revealed in the trial for all to judge. If you wish to be allowed to cover it, then prove your lack of Western bias by denouncing this man's lies in your own press.

BRODY

Is that a threat?

> *Rose shifts nervously in her chair, knocking over a glass.*
> *Duranty rights it and wipes up the spill with his napkin.*

DURANTY

What do you think, Rose? Do you believe this fellow's accusation that the Soviet leadership is intentionally starving its peasants to eliminate a politically undesirable class of people? For, make no mistake, that is the implication of his report.

Rose looks horrified. She hesitates, on the brink of tears.

ROSE

40 No, no, no. . . People are hungry. . .

BRODY

Rose, what about Comrade Zavanova's cousin Firs? He stayed in our flat!

Duranty watches as Rose looks over, confused, at Oumansky.

DURANTY

Would Comrade Oumansky purposely allow people to starve?

BRODY

Leave her alone, Duranty!

Rose looks even more confused and frightened.

OUMANSKY *(gently)*

Please, say whatever you think, Mrs. Brody.

She looks at him, starting to pull herself together.

ROSE

No, of course not. No one would do that. It's inhuman. That's not what is happening. People are hungry. They are malnourished. They are in bread lines. . .

(turning to her husband)

As they are at home right now, Sid. It's no different than the Depression. I don't believe in such evil. And I know the people of America don't either.

Brody looks at her, first with astonishment, then resigna-tion, as she regains her composure while she's talking.

Duranty

Indeed, there is a distinction to be made between malnour-ishment and starvation. How astute you are to point that out, Rose.

(he smiles)

Would you consider it intellectual theft if I use that in my own column?

Rose *(warmly)*

Not at all, Walter. I'd be flattered.

Duranty refills her glass. She smiles at her husband, tak-ing Brody's hand and squeezing it affectionately. He doesn't say anything.

Lights out.

SCENE TEN

Lights up on –

A cold Moscow night

Brody and Rose, bundled in overcoats, stand, shivering on a street corner, clapping their hands together to keep warm.

Rose

Comrade Zavanova told me some terrible news this morn-ing. . . She got a letter from her family in the Ukraine.

BRODY

Firs?

ROSE

He died last week.

BRODY *(looks stricken)*

Starvation?

ROSE *(shakes her head)*

No, his emphysema. You know how bad it was. All that coughing.

BRODY

Everything's terminal on three hundred calories a day.

ROSE

Why do you always have to jump to that conclusion? It's as if you want things to go wrong.

BRODY

Maybe I'm heartbroken.

ROSE *(irritated)*

The whole world is heartbroken.

BRODY

How do you mean that?

> *Before she can answer, Oumansky, also in a heavy coat and fur hat, hurries up to them.*

OUMANSKY

Good evening, comrades. I am sorry to have kept you waiting out here in the cold.

BRODY

It's rather a peculiar place to meet, in front of. . .

> *(gestures)*

OUMANSKY

Lubyanka Prison? They say it is the tallest building in Moscow.

BRODY *(mordantly)*

You can see Siberia from the basement.

OUMANSKY

So you know our jokes now.

BRODY

Some. You have quite a few.

ROSE

Sid has a Russian sense of humor.

> *(ambiguously)*

Very dark.

> *Oumansky notices her discomfort.*

OUMANSKY

Actually, we're going around the corner. I wanted you both to see something.

They stare at Oumansky, wondering what he means. Faintly in the distance, we begin to hear the sound of a Hasidic nigun (humming liturgical music).

(ushering them forward)

You know we could be family.

A small light appears on the scrim.

Just a few steps away from Lubyanka. . . a little shtiebel.

The light on the scrim suddenly expands into a Torah arc out of a Chagall painting. The chants of the unseen Hasidic men grow stronger. They stop, right outside a wooden door.

I know. We cannot go in with a woman. That will be different some day of course. . .

(in a low voice)

Anyway, we don't have to worry. They don't speak English..

(smiles)

Two are my relatives . . . an uncle and a cousin. . . Do you two go to shul in America?. . . Of course not. You are the same as us – Bolsheviks or nearly.

(to Brody)

Where were your parents from?

BRODY

My mother was from a shtetl near Minsk. My father from Odessa.

OUMANSKY

Odessa? My mother's family was from Odessa. So we could be brothers – or cousins at least. Did you know I was Jewish, Sid?

BRODY

I assumed.

OUMANSKY

And you, Mrs. Brody ... or Rose?

ROSE

I came from a large family in the Pale of Settlement. At least sixty or seventy with all the cousins. Every single one of them was killed in pogroms, except for my father and his older sister.

OUMANSKY

I'm sorry.

ROSE

That's why I love the Revolution...

OUMANSKY

Because it made us all equal... It put an end to that...

ROSE *(choked up)*

Yes, it did.

OUMANSKY

So of course we became atheists.

> *He pauses a moment, listening to the dovening.*

Or most of us...

(confidentially)

But it's still not easy for us here ... with so many of us gone from the original Politburo ... Zinoviev, Kamenev, Trotsky ... And now a Georgian who is in charge. What will happen? Sometimes I wonder if he likes us at all... But do not misunderstand. I still believe in the Revolution. It is the most important thing...

The Hasidic voices cry out, as if urging them to join the service.

I have forgotten the prayers. Do you remember?

BRODY

More or less.

OUMANSKY

Maybe you should teach me.

(laughs softly)

No, it's a waste of time. There is something more important to do now. Something urgent.

Brody and Rose watch as Oumansky takes an envelope from under his coat.

About your proposed article on Gareth Jones. Perhaps you didn't mean to be so specific. These details of so-called mass starvation of peasants might be seen as capitalist propaganda by my colleagues. Their reaction could be... unfortunate.

He gestures back toward the unseen doveners.

As you know, my dear Sid, some of us will have to live here when you return to America. I'm sure you would want to reconsider... For all of our sakes.

Brody doesn't say anything.

What do you think, Rose? Do you agree?

She looks over at her husband for a moment, then...   47

ROSE

Yes. Yes, I do.

Oumansky hands the article back to Brody who looks sick to his stomach.

OUMANSKY

You are a good woman.

(to Brody)

You are lucky to have found such a wise and caring wife. And she's given you a beautiful daughter... Good evening, comrades.

He exits. The synagogue image starts to fade from the scrim.

BRODY *(staring at the envelope)*

This is awful. Just awful.

ROSE

Well . . . it's your decision. You don't have to change it if you don't want to.

BRODY *(angry)*

Why didn't you say that to him?

Rose shrugs, conflicted.

Can't you see he was using our religious background to manipulate us?

ROSE

He's Jewish too. Thousands of our people have been murdered.

BRODY

So I'm supposed to lie about the Ukrainian people being murdered? Is that what we came here for?

ROSE

We came here to witness history being made. The greatest leap forward in social justice and equality.

BRODY

Instead we're eyewitnesses to genocide.

ROSE

Maybe you are, but that's not what I see.

They both stand there, increasingly unhappy. Finally. . .

Let's go home. I don't want Comrade Zavanova to be up all night with Emma. She's taking the morning train to Kiev for Firs' funeral.

LIGHTS OUT.

SCENE ELEVEN

LIGHTS UP ON

Long Island, New York. Late afternoon. 1995

Michael and Fortuyn, cocktails in hand, stand on a patio of a huge, baronial era mansion. It overlooks a vast rolling lawn extending all the way to the sandy shore.

MICHAEL *(looking around in awe)*

Stockton did say we wouldn't be in the way if we stayed here.

FORTUYN

We could move in permanently and no one might notice.

> *An elderly woman, DIANA, emerges from the house.*

DIANA

It's true my eyes are dimming, but the hearing hasn't gone yet, gentlemen. I heard a Russian and a Dutch accent. You must be my son's friends.

> *Diana approaches them. She's in her eighties, but looks a decade or two younger and is still a great beauty.*
>
> *(offering her hand)*

I'm Diana Rhodes. Stockton's mother.

MICHAEL *(shaking her hand)*

Michael Duranty.

> *Diana freezes, suddenly staring at him as if he's a ghost. She starts to sway like she's about to faint.*

DIANA *(muttering to herself)*

No ... it can't be.

> *Fortuyn darts closer and puts his arm around her, steadying her.*

DIANA *(to Michael)*

Stockton never mentioned your last name... I ... I wonder if it's possible...?

FORTUYN

Would you like to sit down?

She smiles gratefully, nods. He leads her to a perfectly weathered Adirondack chair and helps her into it.

Pim Fortuyn. It's a pleasure meeting you.

DIANA *(pointing to his drink)*

Is that a gimlet?

He nods.

My favorite. Do you mind? I'll have a fresh one brought out to you.

Fortuyn hands her his drink and she downs most of it surprisingly fast.

Or better yet, a pitcher. Thank you. I feel much improved already.

She turns to Michael who has been watching her somewhat apprehensively.

You were born and raised in the former Soviet Union, Michael?

MICHAEL

Yes. But I've been living in Amsterdam for the last eight years.

She stares at him, really scrutinizing him, searching his face. Then nods.

DIANA *(finally)*

Forgive my rude behavior, but I believe I knew your father. He was British.

MICHAEL

Yes. He was a journalist in Moscow.

DIANA

Walter Duranty.

MICHAEL

I don't really remember him. He left the Soviet Union when I was a young boy and moved to the US. Is that where you met him?

DIANA *(shakes her head)*

I took a tour of the Soviet Union in the 1930's. Your father helped arrange my trip.

FORTUYN

So you were friends?

DIANA

No we weren't. He was quite a snake. Extremely charming and completely amoral.

> *(to Michael)*

I know this isn't my place to say, but you were probably much better off without his influence in your life.

FORTUYN

That's precisely what I tell him all the time.

> *Diana looks at Fortuyn approvingly.*

LIGHTS OUT.

SCENE TWELVE

Lights up on –

The kitchen of Brody's Moscow flat.

Brody is sitting at the kitchen table, an overflowing ash-tray and half empty bottle of vodka in front of him. The air is thick with cigarette smoke. He's staring vacantly out the window at the bleak Moscow street. The sound of the front door opening and Rose entering seems to rouse him. He stubs out his cigarette. Rose enters carrying a small bag of groceries. She starts to cough from the smoke, setting down the bag and hurrying to open a window.

ROSE

Please Sid, all these cigarettes are going to kill you. I managed to get a few lamb chops at the foreigner's store. Let me make you something to eat.

BRODY

I'm not hungry.

(smiling darkly)

I bet I'm the first person to say that inside this godforsaken country all winter.

Rose sighs, starts taking groceries out of the bag.

ROSE

You did the right thing, Sid. I'm proud of you. It's a shame you're not.

Brody leaps up, suddenly about to explode.

BRODY

Proud?! I'm a goddamn liar! I slandered an honest man! I'm an apologist for a brutal, murderous dictatorship. If that makes you proud, Rose, I . . . we. . .

He stops himself, sinks back into his chair.

ROSE

Say it. What you were about to say.

He shakes his head and lights another cigarette.

BRODY

I wasn't going to say anything.

ROSE *(coming over to him)*

Yes you were.

She pulls the cigarette from between his lips and smashes it into the ashtray.

I'm your wife and I'm standing right here in front of you. Talk to me.

He looks up at her, reaching automatically for another cigarette, then stopping himself.

BRODY *(slowly)*

Alright, Rose. If you really want to know. . . I don't understand how you can live here and see what is going on in front of our eyes and somehow refuse to acknowledge it. . . It's fucking genocide!

ROSE

No it's not! How can you say such a thing?!

BRODY *(choking up)*

Because it's the truth and you know it. Deep down inside I know you do.

ROSE

I can't live with you like this. Maybe you don't, but I need to believe in something. I need to get up every morning and think we are making the world a better place for our daughter.

BRODY

Don't you think that's what I want too? But this isn't it. I wish more than anything that it was, but wishing doesn't make it true.

ROSE *(almost pleading)*

It's bad here now, but it's going to get better. All this suffering is for a great cause, Sid. You used to know that. Before the revolution, there was no cause, there was nothing but suffering. Take the cause away and you leave people worse off than they were before they started believing.

BRODY

I'd give anything to think you were right. But even if you are, I can't be part of it. I can't keep lying. . .

> *(he falters, voice cracking)*

. . . I can't, Rose. . .

> *He lets out a sob.*

ROSE *(barely audible, a whisper)*

I understand. Do what you have to. I'm taking Emma and going home to New York.

Brody nods, not looking up, and lights another cigarette.

BRODY

It won't be safe for you here anymore, anyway, with me being an enemy of the people.

He gets up from the table and walks out. Rose busies herself preparing dinner, then abruptly stops. She leans over the sink and starts to cry.

LIGHTS OUT.

_____

SCENE THIRTEEN

LIGHTS UP ON –

Duranty's flat. Late afternoon.

Katya, holding her infant son, is pouring tea for Rose, who stands beside a pram filled with baby clothes.

ROSE

Most of the clothes will be fine for Michael, but there are some dresses as well. I thought you could give them to friends with baby girls.

KATYA

Or sell them. Thank you, Comrade Brody. It is very kind of you.

She picks up a pair of knit booties, fingering the fabric appreciatively.

KATYA

Michael will get spoiled wearing such soft clothes. Then I am afraid he will spend the rest of his life trying to find such nice things again. But they no longer exist here.

ROSE

I am sure by the time he is a big boy, running around, things will improve. And anyway, when he is older he will need rougher clothing meant for boys to play in.

Katya nods, starts taking the clothes out of the pram, and folding each item carefully.

ROSE

Why don't you sit down and rest for a bit, Katya? Have some tea with me so I can say a proper goodbye.

KATYA

I just need to put these clothes away so you can take the baby carriage.

ROSE

But that's for you to keep. Emma is no longer a baby and I won't be having another...

Her voice trails off and she looks away. Before Katya can say anything, the door opens and Duranty enters, flushed with excitement, whistling the Internationale. He heads straight for the hallway, unbuttoning his collar as he goes.

DURANTY *(to Katya without looking at her)*

I need a clean shirt.

She instantly exits down the hall, carrying the baby.

ROSE

Good afternoon, Walter. You're in a fine mood.

He stops, startled to see Rose sitting on the sofa.

DURANTY

Rose! I didn't realize you were here. Forgive me.

He practically skips over and kisses her on both cheeks. 57

Excellent timing, my dear. You are the first to learn of my journalistic triumph. I've one-upped your husband, I'm afraid. Comrade Stalin just gave me a lengthy interview. I've been with him all afternoon! It was a thorough and penetrating discussion, unlike Sid's embarrassing little Soviet press release. Not that I blame him, of course. It takes a seasoned old pro to keep his wits around someone with the enormous power and magnetism of Josef Stalin.

Katya reappears with a pressed shirt. She wordlessly helps Duranty change out of his old shirt and into a new one. He doesn't lift a finger as she ties his necktie.

Drinks will be on the New York Times all night at the Metropole, if you care to join the party.

He puts on his hat and heads towards the door. From another room, the baby cries.

ROSE

Why don't I watch Michael, so you and Katya can celebrate together?

Duranty looks surprised at the very thought.

DURANTY *(to Katya)*

You can come along if you'd like.

Katya shakes her head no.

Suit yourself. Bonsoir, ladies.

DURANTY

He resumes whistling the Internationale as he exits through the front door of the flat.

The baby cries again. Katya starts back to retrieve him.

KATYA

Thank you, but as you can hear, he is a fussy baby.

ROSE

I would have enjoyed looking after him, Katya. Why didn't you want to go?

Katya stops for a beat, looking directly at Rose.

KATYA *(flatly)*

I do not really like Comrade Duranty, so...

She gives a little shrug and walks out. Rose watches her go, takes a sip of tea.

LIGHTS OUT.

SCENE FOURTEEN

LIGHTS UP ON –

The Waldorf-Astoria Hotel, New York. Night

Duranty, in a tuxedo, and Oumansky, in a formal Red Army officer's uniform, stand in front of a small, elegant art deco bar, sipping cocktails. Klieg lights play in the background to a jazz beat à la Paul Whiteman.

DURANTY

They call it a "Manhattan" – three parts Bourbon whisky, one part sweet vermouth with a dash of angostura bitters.

OUMANSKY

In my country it is a woman's drink.

DURANTY

Sid half your country suffer from cirrhosis of the liver and the other half are so demented they can't remember where they are or who they are if they do.

A young woman (DIANA) walks up to them.

DIANA

Korsakoff's Syndrome. Caused by a B-1 deficiency from alcohol abuse. Named after the Russian neuropsychiatrist who identified it, Sergei Korsakoff.

Duranty and Oumansky have turned to see the gloriously attractive young woman in a couture gown. We realize this is the same Diana we met earlier as the elderly mother of Stockton Rhodes. Now she is a gorgeous twenty-one-year-old.

(pointing to the cocktails)

I think I'd like one of those myself.

DURANTY

And risk Korsakoff's Syndrome?

DIANA

I'll take my chances, Mr. Duranty.

DURANTY

You know me?

60   DIANA

Of course I do. You're the guest of honor here tonight. And I've followed your every word since I was a sophomore in high school.

DURANTY *(clearly pleased)*

High school? Very precocious of you, my dear. . .

DIANA

I was only eight when the Russian revolution happened.

> *Duranty takes a good look at her.*

DURANTY

And a very attractive eight I am certain, not to mention a . . . What is your name, if I may be so bold?

DIANA

Diana.

DURANTY *(piecing something together)*

Diana. . . Not Pierson?

DIANA

Yes.

DURANTY

So you're our hostess tonight?

DIANA

Not me, actually. My foundation... But it's because of you that we are all here. Congratulations on your Pulitzer, by the way. Much deserved. And your reporting on the Ukraine was extremely enlightening. You clarified a troubling situation.

DURANTY *(beaming)*

Thank you, Diana.

> *(almost as an afterthought)*

This is...

DIANA *(knows)*

Konstantin Oumansky, Comrade Director of the People's Commissariat of Foreign Affairs. It is also my honor to meet you.

OUMANSKY

Thank you. You said that very well, Miss Pierson. You sound like you know a great deal about the Soviet Union.

DIANA

Only what I have read in Mr. Duranty's work.

DURANTY

Call me Walter.

DIANA *(smiles)*

Walter.

> *Off stage, the music spikes.*

DIANA

I think we're on in a minute.

DURANTY *(nods perfunctorily)*

So you want to learn more about the Soviet Union...

DIANA

Of course. It's the land of the future.

DURANTY

So they say.

DIANA

I thought you agreed... Well, I know it's not perfect. You wrote that yourself. It's very difficult building a utopia.

>*(smiles)*

"You have to break some eggs to make an omelet."

DURANTY *(beams again)*

Yes, indeed...

>*(to Oumansky)*

This young lady is brilliant.

OUMANSKY

Of course. I could have told you that. And beautiful.

>*He nods to her.*

DURANTY

You know, Konstantin, I think the People's Commissariat of Foreign Affairs owes Diana a huge debt for sponsoring this event of friendship between the US and your country.

>*Oumansky nods again, but glances at Duranty wondering what he is up to.*

DURANTY

If you really want to repay her, why not offer her a grand tour of the Soviet Union? Miss Pierson has already said she would like to expand her knowledge beyond what she gets in my paltry columns. Isn't that true, Diana?

DIANA

In fact, I would be very interested.

DURANTY *(to Oumansky)*

How can we deny the lady? I'm certain Soviet authorities at the highest levels would be more than pleased to welcome her.

DIANA

But I wouldn't want one of those "red carpet" tours. I'd like to see the real Soviet Union.

DURANTY

But of course, my dear. Warts and all... I will see to it personally. It will be my mission.

OUMANSKY

No doubt.

ANNOUNCER *(v.o.)*

Ladies and gentlemen, the Waldorf Astoria and the Pierson Foundation welcome you to a celebration of the official recognition of the Soviet Union by the United States of America.

> *The flags of the USA and the Soviet Union are unfurled on the scrim along with portraits of Roosevelt and Stalin.*

With us tonight is the man whose reporting made this reconciliation possible. . . Walter Duranty.

There is deafening applause as. . . .

LIGHTS OUT.

_____

SCENE FIFTEEN

LIGHTS UP ON –

Long Island. Night. 1995.

Michael, Fortuyn and the elderly Diana are having dinner on the patio of the Pierson estate.

DIANA

Thank you for indulging an old woman. I'm sure this wasn't what you had in mind when you accepted Stockton's invitation to visit him at the beach while you were in New York.

MICHAEL

I am sure your son did not expect to be reporting on NATO air strikes over Sarajevo for CNN.

DIANA

No, the call from CNN came as quite a surprise.

MICHAEL

It's a big job in journalism. You must be very proud of him.

Diana pauses thoughtfully before she responds.

DIANA

I'm happy for him. It's what he wanted and he's worked so hard. But I have my qualms about the profession.

MICHAEL

Not every journalist is like my father.

FORTUYN *(dryly)*

Most of them are less clever.

> *Diana laughs.*

DIANA

I'm probably to blame for his career choice anyway. His father was an investment banker which held no allure for a young boy whose mother had what seemed like a very glamorous past. I'm afraid by comparison, my husband's life seemed a little dull, and Stockton grew up determined to follow a different, more adventurous path.

FORTUYN

Interesting or dull – these are superficial observations. I am certain the person you chose to marry had far more substantive qualities... But perhaps not easily discernible or appreciated in youth.

> *Diana looks at him, smiles.*

DIANA

So you're entering Dutch politics?

FORTUYN

Yes. I've managed to find a profession almost entirely devoid of talent or wit.

DIANA

I'm sorry my son hasn't gotten to know you. I really hope he gets the chance.

Fortuyn looks at her curiously. She shakes her head, almost a little shy suddenly.

66

DIANA

It's funny. You remind me very much of someone. A person I admired enormously. And who knew your father, Michael.

MICHAEL

Who is that?

DIANA

A man who wasn't afraid to tell the truth. He wrote a book. . . I think you'd find it interesting, Pim.

FORTUYN

What's it called? I'll get a copy.

DIANA

"The Party Line." It's long out of print. Don't leave without reminding me to give you one. I have a case of them.

LIGHTS OUT.

END OF ACT ONE

> *From a black stage, we hear the haunting voice of Paul Robeson singing "The Anthem of the USSR."*

ROBESON *(v.o.) (singing)*

Long live our Soviet Motherland
Built by the people's mighty hand.
Long live her people united and free. . .

> *As Robeson sings, a giant socialist-realist poster of model workers fades up on the scrim, determined faces beaming out beneath the hammer and sickle.*

. . . strong in a friendship tried by fire
Long may her crimson flag inspire
Shining in glory for all men to see.

> *Diana enters from stage left, illuminated by a spotlight. She is dressed like the workers on the poster, in overalls and sporting a small worker's cap with a red star. And she carries a bouquet of red roses. As she walks across stage, we hear the sound of applause and, in true socialist fashion, she applauds back.*

Through days dark and stormy
When great Lenin led us
Our eyes saw the bright sun of Freedom above. . .

> *Diana exits stage right. The scrim fades.*

LIGHTS OUT.

SCENE TWO

LIGHTS UP ON –

The Metropole Bar. Night

Duranty is sitting at his table, paging impatiently through the Paris Herald Tribune. Oumansky, a few feet off, leans on the bar.

ROBESON *(v.o.)*

... and Stalin our leader
With faith in the people
Inspired us to build the land that we love.

Music ends as the door swings open and Diana enters, still looking quite fetching in her trim-fitting overalls and cap.

DURANTY *(jumps up and bows flamboyantly)*

Welcome to the Metropole, Diana.

(stops bowing suddenly)

Oops, excuse me, not very socialist of me. Anyway, rather dreary here tonight... Normally we get an Eisenstein or a Brecht. Gorky himself has joined us here on occasion, hasn't he, Konstantin?

Oumansky nods perfunctorily.

DIANA

He'd be interesting to meet.

DURANTY

If you like socialist-realist pap... Just kidding. I'd be glad to introduce you. Maxim is a charming fellow. Just don't fall for him because he's Minister of Culture.

Duranty picks up a bottle of vodka sitting on the bar and pours them a couple shots.

That would be unfair since I brought you here.

DIANA

I don't usually fall for people because they're Minister of Culture. It would be a first.

DURANTY

I'm relieved. How are you enjoying the trip so far? Intourist overloading you with ball-bearing factories and pig farms?

He hands her one of the shot glasses.

DIANA

I find it fascinating. I don't get to see that at home.

DURANTY

I imagine not.

They clink glasses and drink.

DIANA

Though it's rather obvious they select these places for foreign visitors. Model factories and all that. It feels a bit staged.

Oumansky looks up, interested.

Like they were putting on a play for me. A woman with the Young Pioneers gave me these overalls and I felt obliged to wear them.

DURANTY *(checking her out)*

Well you look quite the smashing worker hero. They fit you so much better than they do the locals.

(smiles at her)

There's a body type here that's...

Duranty makes a face meant to be flattering to Diana.

DIANA *(pointedly)*

But I've heard your Russian wife is very attractive. You never mentioned you were married.

DURANTY *(displeased)*

Who told you that?

Diana indicates Oumansky.

(looking over at him)

Naughty comrade... Anyway, she's not really my wife. They have this law here. If you live with someone, you have to keep them. Of course, in the early days of the Revolution it was different. They were going to abolish marriage as a bourgeois institution. Just like my old friend Aleister Crowley had done himself.

DIANA *(surprised)*

Aleister Crowley, the Satanist? He's a friend of yours?

DURANTY

Oh, that mumbo jumbo was just an affectation. Drew women to him like a magnet.

(smiles)

We had some wild times in my decadent youth...

DIANA

What ever happened to him?

DURANTY

Crowley? Old rascal's still at it, I think. Last I heard he was staging priapic rituals in a Sicilian nunnery.

DIANA

No. To the laws here.

DURANTY

They were overtaken by natural Russian prudery.

DIANA

But not you.

DURANTY

No. Not me.

> *Duranty studies her, calculating his chances.*

Another vodka?

> *Diana shakes her head.*

DIANA

I'd like to meet your wife.

> *Duranty frowns. Just then the door swings open and Brody enters, looking haggard but determined. He glances around for a split second, then heads straight for Oumansky.*

BRODY

Comrade Oumansky, at last. I've been looking all over for you. I can't believe what's happened.

DURANTY

You seem a bit distraught tonight, Sid?

BRODY *(flatly)*

I'm fine.

DURANTY

You don't look fine... You shouldn't be so hard on yourself. You do have an excuse to be a little under it, you know.

BRODY

Right. Save your phony concern for the Kulaks, Walter.

OUMANSKY

What is the problem, Comrade Brody? I am here.

BRODY *(straining to be polite)*

I'm sure it's an oversight, Comrade. And I'm sorry to trouble you. But I'm not on the press list for the British Engineers trial that begins tomorrow.

OUMANSKY

I'm surprised something of so little significance would be of interest to you. It will be quite a boring discussion of cement construction techniques and so forth.

BRODY

Well, you know us Americans. We love concrete. New York's full of it.

DIANA *(to Duranty)*

What's this about?

DURANTY *(dismissive)*

Engineering technicalities. Nothing of consequence, as Konstantin says.

BRODY *(sharply, to Duranty)*

Right. Sort of like mass starvation. Nothing to look at.

DURANTY

That's not a particularly smart way to get a press pass, Brody.

BRODY

I'll take my chances.

DURANTY *(eyes Oumansky)*

Unless you want a free pass out of here.

BRODY

When I want your advice, I'll ask for it, Comrade Duranty.

DURANTY

That might not be a bad idea, really.

BRODY

So I can learn to be a professional apologist? I guess there's money in that. Or a glamorous prize.

DURANTY

Jealous, are we, Sid?

BRODY

No, just a reporter who wants to do his job tomorrow, by being where I'm supposed to be... How about it, Comrade Oumansky? You're not afraid to have this humble scribe witness a trial of such importance to the future of humanity. Surely there is nothing to hide.

OUMANSKY

Am I to assume you will give an impartial report?

74 BRODY

Test me... But I don't see what you have to worry about in any case. You have to approve whatever I write before it's published anyway.

DIANA *(surprised)*

Really?

DURANTY *(quickly)*

Our hosts are concerned that certain parties deliberately seek to undermine the Soviet experiment with their writing...

(gestures wearily to Oumansky)

... and not without some justification, I'm afraid.

BRODY

Just what parties are you talking about, Duranty?

(points to self)

This party who spent five years writing about socialist labor picnics and fold dances at the Workman's Circle for the Yiddish Daily Forwards? I'm the sort who shouldn't be trusted to report on an attempt to sabotage socialism?

DIANA

Now I'm confused. What is going on?

BRODY *(turns to her)*

Some engineers were sent her by a British company to help build a hydroelectric dam. The completion was delayed and the Soviet government says the engineers deliberately sabotaged it.

DIANA

Why would they do that?

BRODY

To subvert the Five Year Plan.

DIANA

And they're on trial. . .?

BRODY

They allegedly confessed. . . It's my job to verify that.

OUMANSKY

Your job? Isn't that taking it a bit far, Comrade Brody?

DURANTY

Our old friend has become something of a moral crusader, hasn't he?

BRODY

Hardly. I'm just a reporter, unlike some people I know.

　　(to Diana)

Are you a journalist? You should come to the . . .

DURANTY *(interrupts with a laugh)*

Not in the slightest. Diana has better things to do than engage in our tawdry occupation.

　　(disdainfully)

Brody's with one of the wire services.

(checks watch)

Don't forget we have tickets to the Bolshoi tonight... Curtain's in half an hour.

Diana nods peremptorily.

DIANA *(to Brody)*

Thank you for the information.

(extends her had)

I'm Diana Pierson. One of those bourgeois American tourists out for a glimpse of socialist utopia.

BRODY *(frowns)*

The Piersons... of the Pierson Trust? ... I think I saw your picture in the rotogravure.

DIANA

I plead guilty.

BRODY *(grins)*

Sid Brody. Of the Essex Street Brodys.

DIANA

I'd really like to go to that trial tomorrow.

BRODY

Well, it won't be your normal tourist thing. That's for sure.

OUMANSKY

You are scheduled for the metallurgical factory, madame. The responsible leaders will be very disappointed.

DIANA *(suddenly determined)*

After that.

BRODY *(to Oumansky)*

Comrade, the lady would like to see the Soviet justice system for herself. I'm certain the Comintern would not want to deny the director of the Pierson Trust such a privilege. President Roosevelt might turn around and rescind his recognition of the Soviet Union.

Oumansky does not look happy.

(nods to Diana)

I'll be pleased to see you there, Miss Pierson.

She smiles. Oumansky glances over at Duranty who doesn't look very happy either.

LIGHTS OUT.

SCENE THREE

LIGHTS UP ON –

Galleria Gorbachev. Night.

The year – 1997 – flashes on the scrim. We are at a book signing – the sound of people audible in the background. But the room is dark except for the center where an easel displays a large reproduction of a book cover with Pim Fortuyn's photo. The title of the book is "Against the Islamization of Our Culture." Fortuyn himself is seated at a table, signing stacks of books. Michael approaches the table with Stockton Rhodes.

FORTUYN *(without looking up)*

I just signed a book for a Somali woman who told me she emigrated to the Netherlands to escape oppression, only to discover it growing like a weed here. She asked me why our country is letting this happen. I told her an abundance of tolerance would be the politically correct answer. But political correctness is a poison, not so slowly eating away at liberalism from the inside.

> *Finishing the last book in a stack, he looks up at Michael and the young and good-looking Stockton.*

(flirting)

Are you cutting to the front of the line?

MICHAEL

No, no, no. This is Stockton Rhodes. Remember I told you he'd be visiting from New York this week?

FORTUYN

If I'd known how handsome he is, I certainly would have paid more attention.

STOCKTON

We actually did meet once, briefly, years ago at an opening at this gallery. Michael introduced us. You were on your way out even though the opening was just starting.

> *Fortuyn looks at him, shakes his head.*

FORTUYN

Hmmm. I typically remember anyone I want to fuck.

> *Stockton looks embarrassed.*

MICHAEL *(a little tightly)*

It was the night you and I first met, so perhaps you were distracted. Unlike tonight, apparently.

FORTUYN

As you see, young man, a world without political correctness makes people uncomfortable. But lack of freedom is far more uncomfortable in the long run, wouldn't you agree?

MICHAEL *(softly, with sadness)*

For you, it is.

FORTUYN *(emphatically)*

For everyone.

> *(to Stockton)*

You are the budding young TV star. With such a pretty face, no wonder.

STOCKTON

I'm a journalist.

MICHAEL

He's too modest to say that he's the new anchor at CNN.

> *Fortuyn laughs.*

FORTUYN

The masters of quid pro quo. Write something to support the narrative and you get exclusive access. Michael's father was a pioneer in the field.

> *Stockton looks sympathetically at Michael who merely smiles.*

MICHAEL *(to Fortuyn)*

I imagine that's why I put up with you. Atoning for my father's sins.

FORTUYN

In that case, I must express a qualified degree of gratitude for the man.

> *He takes Michael's hand and kisses it with obvious affection, then turns back to Stockton.*

FORTUYN

I don't suppose your network is particularly interested in a homosexual former Marxist professor who warns about the conflict in our Dutch constitution between Article 1, prohibition of discrimination, and Article 7, freedom of speech. Although it should be.

STOCKTON

Surely the two can coexist. As they have for decades. It's just a constant balancing act.

FORTUYN

If you believe that, you have relegated liberty to a mere privilege, not an absolute right. You are throwing it away. And you are on the wrong side of history.

> *Stockton shakes his head. Fortuyn reaches for another stack of books.*

FORTUYN

Don't look so glum. That doesn't disqualify you as a sodomy partner later tonight. All the more reason to enjoy while we still can.

He winks at Stockton and returns to signing books.

Lights out.

_____

SCENE FOUR

Lights up on –

A commisariat office in Moscow. Late Night.

An anxious Brody sits opposite Oumansky in an uncomfortable chair.

BRODY

I would hope you could reconsider.

OUMANSKY

It's a little late for that, Comrade Brody... Or should I say Mister Brody? I have no choice. A directive has come from above. Your behavior at the trial of the British engineers made everything clear. You are no longer considered an impartial member of the press. Certain parties even suspect you are a Western agent yourself.

BRODY *(aghast)*

What?

OUMANSKY

Frankly, I can understand their thinking. Still, I argued on your behalf and was able to achieve...

BRODY

Achieve what? I'm not a spy. I'm a reporter for the United Press and you know it.

Oumansky doesn't say anything.

Look, this is ridiculous.. I was merely trying to do my job. I can't be a propagandist. You know how things are going here.

OUMANSKY *(flatly)*

The Soviet Union goes from triumph to triumph.

BRODY *(appalled)*

Oh, come on. You told me yourself at the synagogue that...

> *Brody suddenly stops himself, glancing around, realizing where they are. Their conversation is no doubt being recorded and Oumansky, who is staring at him, is vulnerable.*

Okay, okay ... sorry.

> *There is quiet for a moment.*

OUMANSKY

So you will not be put on trial, but your visa is revoked immediately. You must leave the Soviet Union within twenty-four hours.

> *(smiles thinly)*

I would advise you take this as an opportunity to go back to America and rejoin your wife and child. You have a nice life there, as you know... Stay away from the Pierson woman. Such class enemies are not for you.

BRODY

Class enemies? I don't have the slightest relationship with Diana. Why are you trying to tell me what to do with my life?

OUMANSKY *(extends his hand)*

Your visa, please.

SCENE FIVE

LIGHTS UP ON –

Brody's flat. Night.

It's nearly empty. All that's left are some wooden packing crates and a couple steamer trunks. Brody is nursing a drink as he packs books into one of the crates. There's a knock on the door. Startled, he spills his drink on himself, curses, and goes to answer it.

BRODY *(trying to pat himself dry as he opens the door)*

Who is...?

He stops mid-sentence at the sight of Diana on his doorstep. He stares at her, then, embarrassed, down at his vodka-soaked shirt.

DIANA *(smiles)*

Drinking alone can be hazardous. Trust me, I've had experience.

BRODY

I find that difficult to believe.

She opens her purse, takes out a handkerchief.

DIANA

May I?

She leans forward and dabs his shirt dry with the cloth.

There. That's better.

84 BRODY

Thank you.

He stands in the doorway, just looking at her.

DIANA *(still smiling)*

May I come in?

BRODY

Oh. . . of course. I'm sorry.

She steps inside, shutting the door behind her. She looks around the empty flat.

DIANA

I hope you don't mind me coming here. I went to your bureau and they told me you were going back to the states. They gave me this address. Looks like I caught you just in time.

BRODY

My train leaves tomorrow.

DIANA

Then I am disturbing you.

Brody shakes his head.

At least let me help.

She begins putting books into the crate.

BRODY

You don't need to do that. They're pretty dusty.

DIANA

Why don't you fix me a drink? We can get this done much faster with an extra pair of hands.

> *Brody smiles, goes off stage into the kitchen, as she continues packing.*

BRODY *(o.s.)*

What can I do for you?

DIANA

Tell the truth. About what's happening here. The famine. The forced deportations. The secret police. The interrogations. . .

> *Brody returns, hands her a drink. She clinks her glass against his and gulps it down like a shot. Hands him back the empty glass.*

BRODY

No one's interested in the truth.

DIANA

I am. You must write a book. If they hear it from someone like you, they'll believe it.

BRODY *(shaking his head)*

If they hear it. . . But they won't. Who's going to publish a book that puts the lie to everything they desperately insist on believing? I'll consider myself lucky to find another newspaper job now that I've left the fold.

DIANA

That's where I can help. Not many people know this, but there are advantages to being an heiress.

She winks at him. Brody grins.

Not only do I know Bennet Cerf extremely well, and loads of other New York editors, but the Pierson estate owns a goodly chunk of Random House. That means me.

BRODY

Look, it's very sweet of you, but I can't. . .

She puts her finger to his lips, silencing him.

DIANA

Ssshh. . .

She leans in close to his face.

It's not a favor. Or if it is, it's from you to me. I can't write. I don't have the experience or the knowledge that you have. But I do have a lot of money and a lot of influential friends. And I want to do something good and important for the world. Won't you help me?

She looks into his eyes, then presses her lips against his. They kiss, slowly at first, and keep kissing. His arms wrap around her.

LIGHTS OUT.

SCENE SIX

LIGHTS UP ON –

Michael's Amsterdam apartment. 2002.

Michael is slumped in a chair in the living room, staring at the T V where a newscaster is speaking in Dutch. A photo of the murdered body of Fortuyn appears briefly onscreen behind the newscaster. Michael flinches but doesn't look away. Stockton reenters carrying a tray with a bottle of mineral water and two glasses. He glances at the TV but the photo of Fortuyn's corpse is no longer there. Instead there is a photo of the alleged murderer.

STOCKTON *(re. newscaster)*

What's he saying now?

MICHAEL

The murderer isn't talking. He's hired a fancy law firm.

STOCKTON

I can't believe, after everything, all the death threats, it was an animal rights activist who shot him.

MICHAEL

What did you expect? Osama bin Laden? The left was angrier with him than the Muslim fanatics . . . even though they'll be the first to have their heads sliced off if Europe becomes Islamic.

STOCKTON

You really think that's going to happen?

MICHAEL

How would I know? Pim thinks. . . He thought. . .

(he starts to sob)

No wonder they killed him. He used to be one of them and. . . and. . .

He can't go on, overcome with tears. Stockton gently puts his hand on Michael's shoulder.

STOCKTON

Would you like me to get you something to eat? You haven't touched anything.

MICHAEL

Not now.

>*He straightens himself up.*

STOCKTON *(after a long pause)*

I know it's not my place to say this, but you should let go a little bit.

MICHAEL

Why?

STOCKTON *(strained)*

He didn't. . .

MICHAEL

What?

STOCKTON

He wasn't. . .

MICHAEL

Faithful to me? He never said he would be.

STOCKTON

You deserved better than that.

>*Michael shrugs. Stockton takes a chair and pulls it closer, opposite Michael.*

STOCKTON

Have you ever considered why you let that happen to you?

MICHAEL   89

What're you, playing Sigmund Freud now? This is Amsterdam, not Vienna.

STOCKTON

Well, then, I might as well say it... It seems to me you let Pim treat you just the way your mother let your father treat her.

MICHAEL *(explodes with rage)*

Jesus Christ!

> *(jumps to his feet)*

You're comparing Pim Fortuyn to Walter Duranty?... The most honest man I have ever met to the biggest liar? Everything my father said was a lie. Letting tens of thousands of Ukrainians starve to death for his own career. What could be more contemptible than that? If he had been a Communist, there might have been some justification, but he didn't believe in anything other than himself. He just thought Russians were pathetic Slavs incapable of ruling themselves democratically or even finding a piss hole without some supreme leader to point their prick in it... We deserved Communism.

STOCKTON

Duranty wasn't a Communist?

MICHAEL

Of course not. You CNN people should know that better than anyone – not reporting Saddam's rape rooms and torture chambers so you could keep your cameras in Iraq. It was all about access for you and it was all about access for my father.

>*(he slumps back in his chair, spent)*

Until the New York Times finally got around to firing him. Who knows why?

STOCKTON *(after a beat)*

Would you like me to leave?

MICHAEL *(unsure)*

Suit yourself.

>*Both men sit there.*

MICHAEL *(finally)*

Why did you come here, Stockton?

>*No answer. They sit there another moment.*

STOCKTON

I'll leave.

MICHAEL

No, stay... For now, stay... I need to get through this.

>*He reaches out for Stockton's hand.*

>>>*LIGHTS OUT.*

SCENE SEVEN

>*LIGHTS UP ON –*

>*Patio of Pierson estate. Long Island. Afternoon.*

The young Diana and a slightly older friend, CONSTANCE, sit in the Adirondacks chairs, sunning themselves.

DIANA

He should be here any minute. How do I look?

CONSTANCE

Disgustingly alluring, as usual. No normal man could resist you.

DIANA

Sid's got weightier things on his mind.

CONSTANCE

Well, if you can't distract him, no one can.

DIANA

I don't want to distract him, Constance. I want to help him.

CONSTANCE

Yes, I know, darling. You want him to write some deeply important, earth shattering tome that will open the world's eyes and which of course shall be dedicated to you.

DIANA *(laughs)*

You're such a cynic and I wouldn't have you any other way. But when you hear what Sid has to say about the Soviet Union, about the lies we are being fed daily, even you may find yourself getting passionate about something significant.

CONSTANCE

I'll be all ears, but don't hold your breath.

As she speaks, Brody steps out onto the patio.

BRODY

Didn't mean to sneak up on you, but I heard your voice and followed the sound. I think the butler was appalled.

Diana jumps up and rushes over to him.

DIANA

You found the house easily enough?

BRODY *(smiles)*

Yes, as it happens, your chauffeur is familiar with the route.

DIANA *(embarrassed)*

Of course. I'm just so pleased you're here.

CONSTANCE

So am I. Now we can finally talk about something else.

DIANA

Sid, I'd like you to meet my oldest and rudest friend, Constance Bucknell. Constance, Sid Brody.

Brody goes over to greet her, shakes her hand.

BRODY

Good to meet you.

CONSTANCE

I'm not yet prepared to say the same about you, but I'm keeping a somewhat open mind. As open as it gets. I don't know exactly what sort of spell you cast on Diana over there in Russia. At least you don't look like Rasputin. But she's much less fun and far too serious since she met you.

DIANA

Constance!

CONSTANCE

It's true. I'm not saying it's all your fault, Sid Brody. But I will hold you responsible for making her happy while you're here.

(she stands up)

Now, if you'll excuse me. They've promised to deliver a pitcher of gimlets to my balcony.

She points to an upstairs terrace in a distant wing of the mansion.

CONSTANCE

Should hold me over until cocktail hour. If I can find my way back, that is.

She departs ostentatiously, leaving Diana and Brody alone.

DIANA

And I bet you thought the drinking started early in Moscow.

Brody looks around at the seemingly boundless property.

DIANA *(embarrassed)*

I know. It's an awful lot, isn't it? I've tried to sell it with the proceeds going to charity, but in this economy, no one can afford to buy it.

BRODY

You don't need to apologize to me for being rich.

DIANA

I believe the proper term is filthy rich.

BRODY

Just remember, you said it. Not me.

DIANA

It's nice here though, isn't it?

> *Brody nods.*

DIANA

And peaceful. No distractions. You could get a lot of work done.

> *Brody looks at her curiously.*

BRODY

Are you proposing something?

DIANA *(in a nervous rush)*

OK. . . That you stay here and write your book.

BRODY

My book?

DIANA

The book you are meant to write. The book that people need to read. The truth. So we don't ever make the same mistakes here.

> *Brody starts to shake his head. She puts a finger to his lips, just like once before.*

Wait. Just let me finish. In New York, you're going to be surrounded by people and institutions determined to stop you. Time will pass, memories will erode, and before you know it, you'll have lost the freshness and sense of urgency something this big requires.

He takes a step back, sits down in a chair, absorbing what she's saying.

Here, you'll have as much solitude as you need, no distractions, and a sympathetic ear whenever you need one.

He looks up at her, moved by the offer.

BRODY *(emotional)*

Really? You'd do that for me? I hope your faith in me isn't misplaced.

Diana leans over and kisses him on the cheek.

DIANA

I know it isn't. And I'm not just doing it for you. The book needs to be written.

He grabs her hands, squeezing them tightly. Then he pulls her down and kisses her again, this time on the mouth.

LIGHTS OUT.

SCENE EIGHT

LIGHTS UP ON –

Metropole Bar. Night.

The place is empty except Duranty, sitting alone, drumming on his table.

DURANTY *(calling out to an invisible bartender)*

Don't try pouring any of that cheap swill that smells like gasoline. Do you know who's coming here, Mitya?... Cecil B. DeMille. You know who that is? Paramount Pictures? The King of Hollywood?

There's no answer.

Of course you don't, you ignorant... whatever... here in the land that time forgot...

*Duranty sighs, goes back to drumming on the table, when the door swings open and Oumansky enters with a bald man in his fifties, wearing a cravat—*CECIL B. DEMILLE.

(springs to his feet)

Mr. DeMille... Welcome to the Metropole.

For a moment DeMille stares at him, confused. Who is this? Oumansky whispers in his ear.

DEMILLE

Ah, yes... of course. Mr. Duranty. What a pleasure. I was told you might be here.

DURANTY *(as they shake)*

You can call me Walter.

DEMILLE

Cecil then...

DURANTY *(ushering him to a seat as Oumansky retreats discretely to a corner)*

I trust you've been getting the red carpet treatment here in the land of the future.

DEMILLE

I've been meaning to get here for years. Unfortunately work intervened. But I always felt I knew what was going on from your dispatches. I'm one of your greatest fans.

DURANTY

And I yours, of course. I thought your new Cleopatra was brilliant!

DEMILLE *(surprised)*

They showed it in Moscow?

DURANTY

Paris.

> *(confidentially)*

I can't stay cooped up in this place all the time, you know.

DEMILLE *(frowns)*

I'm finding it quite interesting here. This country has great spirit.

DURANTY

Yes, the Russian soul.

DEMILLE

And socialism. Do you think it works?

DURANTY

In some ways.

> *DeMille looks disappointed.*
>
> *(quickly)*

In many ways, actually. . . This is a great story. And nobody's told it on film. As I told you in that letter, I've been working on a few ideas.

> *(glances toward Oumansky, more confidentially)*

I'd be willing to come to Hollywood if need be.

> *DeMille studies Duranty who seems a tad overeager, but the mogul has seen this before.*

I've been sort of . . . outgrowing journalism.

DeMILLE *(nods)*

The American public might be interested in a movie that told the truth about the Soviet adventure. Of course, it would need to have a dramatic, personal story. . .

DURANTY

Absolutely. Personal. . . As a matter of fact, for a long time I've thought the way to go . . . would be a love story set against the background of the Revolution.

DeMILLE *(amused)*

He and she on a tractor. . . Comrade Oumansky, what do you think?

> *(signaling him to come over)*

You're the expert.

DURANTY *(as Oumansky joins the table)*

It's back in the early Revolution when they're building the hydro-electric plants. Two model workers – gorgeous young kids – fall in love. It could be very visual. Those dams are amazing. They might even let us shoot there.

> *He glances at Oumansky who nods.*

DeMILLE *(flatly)*

Where's the conflict?

DURANTY

Well... you know... he could be from the Steppes and she's... from Byelorussia. Thousands of miles apart. They practically don't speak the same language... Clark Gable and Myrna Loy.

DEMILLE

You would have Americans playing Russians? I don't think that's believable.

DURANTY

You did it in Cleopatra.

DEMILLE

That was ancient Egypt. You want something that has the feel of now for this... but with a western hero. American, British... Someone the audience could identify with. Someone who risks all for his ideals. That's what makes a movie.

Duranty searches for an idea but with no immediate luck.

That's okay. You'll think of something and let me know when I'm back home.

He turns to Oumansky – time to move on.

DURANTY *(afraid he's bombing)*

No, no, no. Wait... Here's one... Very personal... A solitary hero battling the odds to find the truth.

DeMille hesitates, listening.

DURANTY

There's supposed to be a famine in the Ukraine – a forced famine – but no one knows for sure. And no one in the Moscow press corps is allowed to go to find out. But this one young journalist... against all odds... defies everyone – the Soviet authorities – and sneaks off on a train to the Ukraine at great personal risk... where he discovers thousands of people are starving to death and...

OUMANSKY *(stunned)*

That's Gareth Jones!

DURANTY

Well...

OUMANSKY

You wrote yourself he was a liar. And the famine was an exaggeration. It never happened.

DEMILLE *(taken aback)*

Yes, I saw that too. In the article you wrote in the Times.

DURANTY *(caught)*

Yes, maybe, but, uh ... it doesn't have to be that famine. And it doesn't have to be Jones. It could be anybody.

> *(laughs nervously)*

Smith?... Smith? Jones?... Forget that one. It's no good. Too controversial. And depressing. Who wants a movie about starving peasants anyway?

DEMILLE

Good point.

> *(stands, to Oumansky)*

I have to call my London distributor. You must have a phone somewhere I can use...

Oumansky nods, stands.

DURANTY *(gets up too)*

I have plenty of other ideas. That Gareth Jones thing was, you know... a joke.

DEMILLE

I understand... If you get to Hollywood, contact my office. Nice to meet you, Mr. Duranty.

> *He signals to Oumansky who follows him to the door. They exit, leaving Duranty standing there. He sits back down at the table.*

> *LIGHTS OUT.*

SCENE NINE

> *LIGHTS UP ON –*

> *A Manhattan penthouse apartment. Night.*

> *The skyline is outlined against the scrim. Brody and Diana, dressed nicely, hang their coats on a rack.*

BRODY

Maybe I shouldn't mention the book. We don't want a repetition of the last party.

DIANA

Babbits... This is an intimate dinner for the literary crowd. Some of them may even know better. Just keep cool.

BRODY

I'll try.

She gives him a reassuring kiss on the cheek as Constance, the hostess, hurries up to them.

CONSTANCE

First ones here – the Long Island set.

(gives them kisses)

What're you drinking?

(gestures towards a bar)

I recommend the gin fizz.

DIANA

Perfect. I'll have six.

BRODY

Ditto.

CONSTANCE *(to Brody)*

So how's the book going?

BRODY (glancing at Diana)

Chugging right along.

DIANA

Generating a little advance controversy. From people who've never been there.

CONSTANCE *(smiles as the doorbell rings)*

I can't wait to read it.

She opens the door to reveal Mark, Brody's old friend from the ocean liner farewell. But he's looking a lot older and a lot better dressed in an ascot and dinner jacket.

What timing. Here's someone you both just have to meet. Mark Kravitz, director of the new hit play about the garment workers' strike. It's so authentic you almost want to smash the bosses yourself.

> *Mark and Brody stare at each other.*

Mark, I'd like you to meet my good friend Diana Pierson and her friend Sid Brody, the journalist.

BRODY *(trying to be friendly)*

Hello, Mark. Congrats on the new play.

MARK *(forced)*

Hello, Sid. Good to see you after all this time.

> *(nods toward Diana)*

I see you've come up in the world.

BRODY

You too. No more Christopher Street walk-ups, I imagine.

CONSTANCE

You know each other?

MARK

Oh, yes. . . For a long time. I saw Sid off at the boat before he went to the Soviet Union and came back to tell us all it's a totalitarian hellhole.

> *Brody blanches. Diana gives Mark a look.*

I read his Moscow dispatches. Not exactly what you'd expect from a man who once covered the labor beat for the Daily Forwards.

(turns to Brody)

What's going to be in this book of yours we've been hearing so much about? How Stalin raped a thousand Georgian children in a Tblisi kindergarten? Or was it the Ukraine?

DIANA *(bristling)*

What's that supposed to mean?

MARK *(smirking)*

Just kidding.

DIANA

There really was forced starvation in the Ukraine. It's all in Sid's book.

MARK

Well, in that case.

BRODY

You don't really want to know, do you?

MARK

Why not? Who wouldn't want an inside view from the man who's been to see the future and now wants to betray it?

Brody takes a breath, trying to restrain himself. But it's clear he's having a lot of difficulty.

So enlighten me.

BRODY

If that's what you want.

MARK

Oh, I do.

CONSTANCE *(sotto voce)*

Uh oh.

BRODY

Well, one of the key chapters is actually about my return from the Soviet Union. It concerns a phenomenon right here in Manhattan I call "Penthouse Bolsheviks."

DIANA *(suddenly apprehensive)*

I think maybe this is not the right time.

BRODY *(ignoring her)*

It's about all the millionaires and beautiful people, literati and artistes, would-be and otherwise, who hang out at ritzy Manhattan dinner parties insisting socialism is the answer, when the real citizens of the Soviet Union spend their lives freezing in Siberian labor camps... unless they've died of starvation first.

> *(growing more intense in spite of himself)*

Almost everyone we know has been living like an ostrich since 1918, pretending the Russian Revolution was the be all and end all of civilization so we could keep our jobs, drink martinis with some overfed phony Marxist at the New Yorker, or get our next play put up at a so-called people's theatre where rich audiences pay big ticket dollars to feel good about their social consequences, while ordinary people stand outside on breadlines.

DIANA

Sid...

BRODY

It's outrageous, if you ask me.

MARK

Well, fuck you.

BRODY *(going right on)*

Worse than that. It's morally reprehensible. I can't see how you all live with yourselves. Stalin's not a hero of the working classes. He's a dictator, a torturer and a mass murderer. You don't believe me? Ever been inside the bowels of Lubyanka Prison? Ever see peasants starving by the side of the road in the Caucuses with their stomachs distended, fighting over scraps of squirrel meat covered with flies? Ever been to a forced labor camp in the Gulag where people are beaten with birch branches until their skin turns inside out and their bones shatter into little white bits like broken clam shells on a beach? Well, come with me. . .

CONSTANCE *(coolly)*

I don't think we will, Mr. Brody. . . Diana, I think you should escort your friend home if you don't mind, before my other guests arrive. . . I'm sorry, Mark.

> *Diana looks at Brody, who is now completely overwrought, and realizes she has no choice. She starts to escort him out.*

BRODY *(distraught, to Diana)*

I guess I fucked up. I. . .

> *They disappear off stage. Mark and Constance watch them go.*

MARK *(to Constance)*

Poor bastard. He's jealous. Duranty already debunked this Ukrainian nonsense in the Times. And he's got a Pulitzer.

LIGHTS OUT.

SCENE TEN

LIGHTS UP ON –

Duranty's flat.

Afternoon light streams in on Duranty at his desk, still in bathrobe and slippers, drinking coffee. Harold Denny stands beside him, holding a note pad.

DURANTY *(sounding a little hollow)*

Glad the Times hired you, Denny. I've been practically begging them to bring on a strapping young cub like yourself. Quite frankly, I'm getting too old to run around this frozen hellhole at the whim of the Soviet press office. Moscow used to be different. The Wild West. Stories everywhere. They showed up at my doorstep. Now, I'm expected to screw on the old leg and drag myself to the cable office at two A.M. With a report on grain allotments for the Caucasus.

DENNY

With all due respect, the famine is important news.

Duranty holds out his cup as Katya enters with a pot of coffee and refills it.

DURANTY *(chuckles)*

Of course it is... Listen, young man, if you play your cards right and follow in my admittedly slowing footsteps, one day all this will be yours.

(gestures around the flat)

It might not seem like much, but you can't imagine the conditions I worked in when I first got here. None of this came for free.

There's a loud rapping at the front door.

(yelling)

Katya!

Katya hurries to the door and opens it to reveal a tall man dressed completely in black with a shaved head and carrying a black valise. It's Duranty's old friend, ALEISTER CROWLEY. Crowley stares at Katya with interest.

CROWLEY

I think I shall ask Walter if I may borrow you for a while.

Katya looks at him uncomprehendingly, but Duranty, hearing Crowley's voice, leaps up.

DURANTY

Only if you promise to return her in one piece, you degenerate old beast. She's the mother of my offspring.

Katya steps aside as Crowley bursts in and the two men embrace.

CROWLEY

You're a father, Walter? Will miracles never cease?

DURANTY

No one was more surprised than I, but what the hell?

> *Denny listens somewhat uncomfortably, but is eyeing*   109
> *Crowley curiously.*

> *(noticing)*

Forgive my eroding manners, Denny. Allow me to introduce you to "the Wickedest Man in the World," "the Great Beast," "Frater Padurabo," . . . Aleister Crowley!

> *Denny takes a step back in astonishment as Crowley*
> *moves forward to shake his hand.*

CROWLEY *(grinning)*

I won't bite.

DURANTY

Liar.

> *Denny extends his hand gingerly.*

DENNY

Harold Denny, New York Times.

DURANTY

Katya, bring us this instant the copious amounts of vodka and caviar I know you have stashed away for your personal consumption. My old friend is a man of large appetites.

> *Katya hurries out of the room.*

It's been more than a decade, Aleister. What on earth, or in your case elsewhere, brings you all the way to Moscow from undoubtedly warmer climes?

Crowley ceremoniously sets his valise on the dining table.

CROWLEY

110   Perhaps you should sit down for this.

Denny still stands there awkwardly, not wanting to interrupt, but unsure what to do. The other two ignore him completely as Duranty pulls out a chair and sits. Crowley removes his topcoat with a flourish and carefully lays it over the back of another chair. Then he opens the valise and takes out a velvet cap embroidered with magical symbols, which he puts on his head. From off stage comes the sound of a toddler playing and shouting. Next, Crowley removes an ornately carved wooden box also covered with strange symbols painted in gold leaf.

DURANTY

A tad early in the day for this sort of thing, isn't it? At least, let's wait for the vodka.

(calling out)

Katya!

On his call, Katya can be heard off stage speaking harshly in Russian. The child's shouts cease. Duranty shrugs, looking a little embarrassed by the domesticity. Katya enters with a tray of food and drink and sets it on the table. She pours vodka and hands out the glasses.

Alright, you've aroused my curiosity. What's in that box, then, Crowley?

CROWLEY

Your wife's heart. And pancreas.

Denny chokes on his vodka. Katya drops the bottle she's holding. It shatters all over the floor. She stares in shock at Duranty, who himself appears only mildly surprised.

DURANTY *(to Crowley)*

Never told her I was married, I guess.

Denny is still sputtering.

(to Denny)

A youthful indiscretion. In Paris. You know how that is.

Denny shakes his head no.

CROWLEY *(to Katya, soothingly)*

No need to fret. He's not anymore, my dear.

(to Duranty)

I regret to inform you that our beloved Scarlet Woman, Jane Cheron Duranty, has departed from this mortal plane.

DURANTY *(frowns)*

What happened?

CROWLEY

It was very peaceful, on the wings of her lover, opium. A week ago. But fear not, I performed all the necessary rituals to ensure that our Dark Lord, Satan, will welcome her to the netherworld with open arms and girded loins.

Duranty takes a swig of vodka, looks wistful.

DURANTY

Thank you for that. Although we drifted apart these last years, we did have some interesting times, Jane and I.

> *Katya bursts into tears and runs out of the room. Denny is gaping at the men in disbelief.*

DENNY

Does the New York Times know you were married to a drug addict in Paris?!

DURANTY

They never asked.

CROWLEY *(clearing his throat)*

There's just one last matter of business to attend to.

> *He opens the box and takes out two glass vials filled with murky brown fluids.*

I boiled the organs, pureed them, and prepared a distillate from that.

DURANTY

To what purpose, may I ask?

CROWLEY

For you to consume, of course. So that the deceased may pass on to you her many admirable qualities – her strength of character, her adventurous spirit.

> *He opens the vials and pours some of each into Duranty's glass. Off stage, the toddler's cries again erupt. Crowley listens with interest as he slides the glass over to Duranty.*

There's more than enough for two. I should think your heir would benefit from a dose of Jane as well.

Duranty nods. To Denny's horror, Duranty picks up the glass and drinks it down in a shot, wiping his mouth with the back of his hand.

DURANTY

Surprisingly sweet, since she wasn't. I think the boy could handle it.

(calling out)

Michael! Come here!

As Crowley fills another glass, Denny begins to retch. He rushes to the front door, flings it open and runs out into the hall, followed a second later by the sound of vomiting.

Ah well, I've been ready to leave the Times for awhile anyway.

LIGHTS OUT.

SCENE ELEVEN

LIGHTS UP ON –

The Brodys' old Lower East Side apartment. New York.

Rose is ironing, listening to some blues on the radio, when there is a knock on the door. She frowns, not knowing who it could be, but props up the iron and goes to the door to open it. Brody is standing there.

ROSE

Oh, Sid, it's you. . . I thought you were coming at eleven.

BRODY

I thought I'd get here a little early.

ROSE

Oh. . . well, Emma's still asleep. Do you want me to wake her?

BRODY

No, don't. . . Not yet.

> *Brody walks around the apartment – his old apartment – looking around tentatively at a place so familiar and yet so foreign.*

ROSE *(probing)*

You came in from Long Island?

> *Brody nods.*

ROSE

You must have gotten up pretty early yourself.

BRODY *(grins)*

Five thirty. . . I got the first train.

> *Rose looks at him. What's this about?*

ROSE

You want a cup of coffee?

BRODY

Thanks.

ROSE *(as she goes for it)*

How's your book coming?

BRODY

Everybody asks me that.

(laughs softly)

It's creating quite a ruckus for something that hasn't been published yet.

ROSE

I know. I heard you got into a big fight at a fancy dinner party.

BRODY

Never even made it to the first course. I don't think I'm meant for fancy parties. . . Who told you? Mark?

ROSE *(nods)*

He's quite the theatrical big shot these days.

BRODY

He was always talented.

ROSE

Not as talented as you.

BRODY

Well, thank you. . . Do you think I've betrayed it?

ROSE

No. Not at all.

> She hands him his coffee.

BRODY

I'm not exactly a friend of the revolution anymore.

> *(gestures to the couch)*

Mind if I sit down with this?

ROSE

You won that couch at the Workman's Circle raffle. You should be able to sit down on it.

BRODY *(examining it as he sits)*

That feels like a long time ago. It could use a new cover.

ROSE

Who couldn't?

> *She sits opposite him.*

ROSE *(after a moment)*

So how is it for you out there?

BRODY

Southampton? Okay, I guess, but it's not exactly what I'm used to.

ROSE *(smiles)*

You probably had to buy yourself some new clothes.

BRODY

A few things. . . I'm still not very comfortable in them.

ROSE

I can imagine it's not easy for you. And it's not just the clothes.

BRODY

No.

ROSE

It's been hard for me too. . . in a different way.

BRODY

What do you mean?

ROSE

When I came back, I started to see I might have been wrong about a few things. You're not the only one who changed.

Brody looks at her, surprised.

ROSE

Well, not changed exactly. Just became a bit more honest with myself. It's a lot easier to breath over here than it ever was in the Soviet Union. I admit it now. But I can't talk to anyone about it because I'm not as brave as you are.

BRODY

I don't feel so brave.

ROSE

Oh, but you are. Compared to most people... And a little headstrong too.

BRODY

I guess I am.

ROSE

Besides, I have Emma. And we live down here on the Lower East Side. You know how it is... If I started telling the truth about the communists, I'd lose the few friends I have.

Brody laughs. She's right.

You know what I think, Sid? We don't really change. Not in our cores. The world changes and some people adapt and others don't. It took me a long time, but I'm getting there.

Starting to, anyway. . . I wasn't always as honest about it as you were.

BRODY *(smiles)*

Or as headstrong.

> *Rose laughs. They sit there a moment.*

ROSE

Where are you going to take Emma?

BRODY

I was thinking about the Bronx Zoo.

ROSE

That's a long way on the subway.

BRODY

I know.

> *(smiles)*

I think she can make it. . . Want to come with us?

> *She hesitates, then. . .*

ROSE

Okay, yes. . . I would, yes.

> *Brody and Rose sit together a moment.*

LIGHTS OUT.

SCENE TWELVE

LIGHTS UP ON –

Fortuyn's Amsterdam home. 1997.

Moonlight illuminates Fortuyn's bathroom – a simple but elegant white-tiled room. Fortuyn is immersed in the bath watching a television mounted on a wall. The footage he is watching on TV is simultaneously being projected onto the scrim so the audience can watch as well. It's a debate between Fortuyn and a socialist member of the Dutch parliament.

MODERATOR *(on TV)*

Mr. Fortuyn, would you like to explain to Marcel van Dam why Islamization is a threat to our culture?

FORTUYN *(on TV)*

Yes, I have elaborated on that part in my book with three parts. The first part is the separation of church and state. In our culture it took four centuries to accomplish that. And that cost many a little torrent of blood. Why is this so important?

Michael enters the bathroom fully dressed.

FORTUYN

Come in. The water's nice and hot.

Michael watches the TV as he undresses.

FORTUYN *(on TV)*

Because it safeguards the public domain from direct intervention by ideologies, philosophies, churches. We therefore have put the filter of parliamentary democracy in between.

MICHAEL *(taking off his pants)*

You look handsome.

FORTUYN

So do you.

> *He splashes some bath water at Michael who smiles.*

FORTUYN *(on TV)*

There is freedom of expression connected with it, freedom of the press, and human rights. What I see here, let me finish my argument, I note that in many Muslim countries the relation between church and state is an extremely problematic one...

> *Michael gets into the tub, still watching.*

...and that in many Muslim countries they have absolutely no interest in it.

> *As Fortuyn's debate opponent begins to speak, Michael picks up the TV remote.*

MICHAEL

Can we turn it off now? I was there, I saw it all.

> *Fortuyn smiles and nods as Michael turns off the TV and the image on the scrim disappears.*

FORTUYN

I know it makes you uncomfortable when I'm attacked. Even by a pathetic frightened career politician like van Dam.

MICHAEL

He called you...

FORTUYN *(interrupting)*

". . . an extremely inferior human being."

> *Fortuyn laughs.*

MICHAEL

It's not funny. Why do you have to be so confrontational?

> *Fortuyn starts washing Michael's back.*

MICHAEL

It's dangerous for you. And for what? You are just making enemies.

FORTUYN

Do you think I'm right, though?

> *Michael hesitates, closing his eyes as Fortuyn leans in, alternately kissing and scrubbing his back.*

MICHAEL *(finally)*

Mostly yes, but. . .

FORTUYN

I stand for this country. For what has been built here over centuries. For the freedom that lets the two of us do what we want in this bath and still be respected members of society. But we are facing a fifth column, make no mistake. The writing is on the wall. Now in my beloved liberal Netherlands, I must hear that Allah is great, which is perfectly fine, but that I am a dirty pig and you are a Christian dog. That is what they say and our politicians think that is okay. They accept being walked over, but I cannot be silent and let that happen anymore. It is not about me. It's about our children. Our grandchildren. They must have the same freedoms we do. So I speak up and confront people. I cannot do it any other way and I will not do it any other way. You say it is dangerous and you are right. So then, I will be finished off.

Maybe so. But the problem will remain. That will remain.

He turns Michael around to face him and kisses him gently but deeply. Michael responds, then finally pulls away and starts to sob. Fortuyn strokes his head.

Michael, I know you don't yet fully agree with me. You go along because you love me and that's good enough for me. Because I know that one day you will.

LIGHTS OUT.

SCENE THIRTEEN

LIGHTS UP ON –

Duranty's Moscow flat. Day.

The furniture is still there, but the books, artwork, all his personal belongings are gone. His corner desk is empty save for an ashtray. Two large crates are stacked neatly against a wall. There is a knock at the front door. Katya enters from off stage and goes to answer it. It's Duranty's successor at the Times, Denny.

DENNY

Good afternoon, Katya. . .

KATYA *(flatly)*

You've come to collect his things.

He nods, smiles a little sheepishly. She gestures for him to enter and points to the crates.

DENNY *(walking in)*

Yes, well. . . I imagine you'll be glad to have these out of your way. More space for Michael to play.

> *Katya shrugs. Denny goes over to the crates and struggles to pick one up.*

> *(obviously straining)*

Not too heavy. . .

KATYA

I help you.

DENNY

No need. I can manage.

> *He staggers towards the front door. Katya hurries over and takes the other side of the crate. Together they carry it across the room.*

Thank you. If we just move them both out into the hall, I've got a dolly to take them downstairs and a car waiting. I'll be out of your hair in a minute.

> *They carry the crate out the front door, momentarily disappearing off stage, then re-entering for the second one.*

And how is Michael? You must bring him to the bureau sometime.

KATYA

For what?

DENNY

It will be fun for him to see a newspaper office. He's getting old enough to learn about what his father does for a living.

They pick up the other crate.

KATYA *(as they carry it)*

124 Then he will only ask where his father is and why he does not see him.

DENNY

I'm sure as soon as Walter is settled and can get visas for both of you, he'll arrange for you all to be together.

Katya shakes her head.

KATYA

You do not know him like I do. He does not care about us.

They exit with the crate, returning on stage a moment later empty-handed. Embarrassed, Denny looks around the room, avoiding Katya's gaze.

DENNY

Of course he does. . . I should let you get back to what you were doing before I intruded. If you need anything at all, Katya. . .

He starts backing out, then suddenly stops, noticing something.

DENNY

Oh. . . I forgot. He asked me to pick up that old samovar. Apparently, he forgot to box it up.

Denny starts across the room to retrieve it when Katya suddenly erupts in fury, screaming.

KATYA

Nyet!! Nyet!! Nyet!!

She runs over to the samovar and stands, arms spread open in front, blocking access.

(shouting)

He gives us nothing! He sends no money! He abandons us! This is only thing left of value. It is Russian. It is mine! He cannot take it! He is monster! Get out of here!!

DENNY

Katya... I...

KATYA *(shrieking)*

Get out!! Get out!!

She picks up the ashtray and throws it at Denny. It whizzes past, just missing him, and crashes to the floor. From off stage, a child starts to cry. Denny backs up towards the door.

LIGHTS OUT.

SCENE FOURTEEN

LIGHTS UP ON –

Diana's Long Island estate

Brody is sitting in one of the Adirondack chairs, looking out at the ocean. Diana comes up behind him, watching him, frowns.

DIANA

Don't look so glum. Your book's being published in a week. It's exciting.

He nods perfunctorily.

All those Penthouse Bolsheviks are going to...

(studies him)

What's wrong? Something's wrong, isn't it?

She continues to look at him. Brody stands.

BRODY

I'm going back to Rose.

Diana contracts, almost gasps.

DIANA *(trying to keep it together)*

I see... Well... I could pretend I'm surprised, but I'm not. I may be young but suddenly I'm feeling very old and experienced. And I don't much like it.

BRODY

I'm so sorry, Diana.

DIANA

I know you are... How will you deal with her being a communist? That should make for some interesting dinner conversation, justifying every bloodthirsty act of Comrade Stalin.

BRODY

She's over that... She says so anyway.

DIANA

And you believe her? She's not just saying that to get you back?

BRODY

I wondered the same thing at first. But I think she's really changed. For the most part, at least... It's difficult for everyone.

DIANA

Yes, that's what you say in your book. It's painful... Well, now it's painful for me.

BRODY

I've been meaning to tell you for a week, but I've been too much of a coward. I know this sounds awful but I don't know how to thank you for everything you've done for me.

(smiles sheepishly)

At least now you won't have to listen to my embarrassing rants in front of your friends anymore.

DIANA

Yes, that's a point. Too bad I usually agreed with them...

(takes a breath)

I think I am going to ask you to leave now. It's better for both of us.

He nods and walks across the patio, toward french doors that lead into the house. He opens them and nearly trips over a stack of cardboard cartons just inside.

I'm sorry. It's your book. I was going to surprise you with a party.

He shakes his head apologetically.

BRODY

I'll take them...

DIANA *(walking over to him)*

It's not necessary.

She pushes the cartons out of the way.

Good luck, Sid. I really mean it. I wish you the best.

Diana gives Brody a heartfelt embrace and runs into the house, exiting the stage.

LIGHTS OUT.

SCENE FIFTEEN

OLDER WOMAN'S VOICE *(FRANCES) (O.S.)*

Walter, will you get out of there? You've been swinging in that thing all day...

LIGHTS UP ON –

A suburban Florida backyard. Day.

A hammock is strung between two palm trees. Duranty, looking rather old and decrepit, sits up suddenly, struggling not to fall out, as a grey-haired, obviously well-heeled woman in pastels approaches – FRANCES.

FRANCES

All you do is lie around waiting for this one to call and that one to call. They never call. You've been waiting for "your friend Mr. DeMille" for four years and he hasn't called once, unless you count when his secretary rang up by mistake looking for Jimmy Durante. What she thought he was doing in Florida, I'll never know... What happened to that column you were supposed to do for the Tampa Advertiser?

DURANTY

They're not interested in foreign policy.

FRANCES

I should imagine not... Well, I thought you were going to go to the market. The ladies will be here for mah-jongg in an hour and I don't have anything to serve... Did you lose the list again?

> *Duranty clumsily stumbles out of the hammock, looking for the shopping list.*

DURANTY *(finding it, relieved)*

Here it is!

FRANCES

Good. Take my car.

> *She hands him keys. Duranty starts off.*

You'll need some money.

> *He stops, nods resignedly.*

You always need money.

> *She takes some cash out of her purse and hands it to him.*

DURANTY

Thank you, Frances.

FRANCES

And give me a kiss.

> *He nods dutifully and kisses her lightly on the lips.*

FRANCES

Bring me a receipt... You know my friend Elizabeth says she heard some Ukrainians are forming a committee to take away your Pulitzer. What do you think of that?

Duranty frowns for a moment.

DURANTY

130   It'll never happen.

FRANCES

That's what she says.

Somewhat reassured, Duranty heads off.

FRANCES *(stopping him)*

Walter. . . Be back in an hour.

He nods obediently and heads off.

LIGHTS OUT.

SCENE SIXTEEN

LIGHTS UP ON –

Michael's Amsterdam Apartment 2002. Night.

The TV news is still being projected on the scrim in the background. The endless loop of Pim Fortuyn footage. Michael is dozing on a couch as Stockton enters from another room (off stage). He looks over at Michael, then quietly retrieves his jacket from a coat rack and slips it on. He walks over to Michael, takes a throw from the back of the couch and gently covers Michael with it. Michael opens his eyes. He sits up abruptly, a little disoriented.

MICHAEL

I must have nodded off. How long have I been asleep?

STOCKTON

About an hour. I bet you haven't slept since it happened.

MICHAEL

Barely.

STOCKTON

When my father killed himself, my mother didn't close her eyes for six days.

MICHAEL *(surprised)*

You never told me he committed suicide. I thought it was an accident.

STOCKTON *(shakes his head)*

That's for public consumption.

MICHAEL

You rarely mention him. Is that why?

STOCKTON

There's not much to say. He was a nice man. A little dull compared to my mother. She sucked all the air out of a room.

MICHAEL

Is that why he did it?

STOCKTON *(shrugs)*

I think he was afraid of boring her. It was his one attempt at some drama. And it meant she could never leave him. But I was just a teenager at the time... What did I know?

MICHAEL *(noticing his jacket)*

You're going?

STOCKTON

I have to be on air in an hour for the morning broadcast in New York.

MICHAEL *(pointedly)*

Will I be upset with you if I watch it on TV?

> *Stockton doesn't answer.*

Before you go, I have something for you.

> *He gets up and starts out of the room.*

> *(exiting)*

Wait...

> *Stockton is alone. He watches a clip of Fortuyn on the TV. Then he walks over to the samovar, examines it. Michael re-enters, carrying a book. He hands it to Stockton, who looks at it, perplexed.*

MICHAEL

It belonged to Pim. Your mother gave it to him.

> *Stockton looks at him, startled.*

STOCKTON

They knew each other?

MICHAEL *(somewhat surprised)*

When we came to New York in '95 and you invited us to your house on Long Island. But then you were called to Sarajevo for the NATO air strikes. She didn't tell you we met?

STOCKTON *(shakes his head)*

I thought she stayed in the city... She was full of secrets...

> *Suddenly, Stockton chokes up, like he's about to cry.* 133
> *Michael puts a hand on his shoulder. Stockton looks*
> *down at the book, unable to speak.*

MICHAEL

"The Party Line." Whenever you're ready.

> *Stockton walks to the front door, clutching the book. He*
> *opens the door and steps out.*

STOCKTON *(turning back)*

When will that be?

> *Michael shrugs. Stockton turns away, shutting the door*
> *behind him. Michael is alone in the middle of the room.*
> *He turns to the scrim where Fortuyn is giving a speech.*
> *The lights dim, leaving only the scrim illuminated. It*
> *freezes on an image of Fortuyn which remains for a*
> *moment until the screen goes black.*

> LIGHTS OUT.

SCENE SEVENTEEN

> *LIGHTS UP ON –*

> *Oumansky's office. Day.*

> *Oumansky is sitting at his desk, reviewing and signing*
> *where necessary a stack of documents. There is a knock*
> *on the door.*

OUMANSKY

Come in.

> *The door opens and Katya enters, a little older and heavier set.*

KATYA *(flatly)*

You wanted to see me.

OUMANSKY

My old comrade, Katya. It's been a few years. Did you think I'd forgotten about you?

> *(not waiting for an answer)*

How is young Mischa? Ten years old? A little man now.

> *Katya stands there. Oumansky gestures for her to sit down. She obeys, unsmiling.*

OUMANSKY

It's not his fault his father is a decadent capitalist criminal who abandoned his wife and child. The Soviet Union looks after its citizens. Mischa will have a bright future. I have assured that.

> *(smiles at Katya)*

I have secured him a place in our Young Pioneers program. He should be ready to leave in a fortnight for the camp in Artek. At the end of the summer, if he does well, he will be placed in a very elite school only for the children of high party officials and heroes of the revolution. But for your sacrifice, Katya, I pulled some strings.

KATYA

No, he cannot go. I did not ask you for any favors.

OUMANSKY

Don't be silly. This will be better for both of you.

Katya shakes her head vehemently and gets up to leave.

OUMANSKY *(annoyed, with an edge)*

You are being selfish and thinking only of yourself. Shame on you.

Katya stops, looks at him.

KATYA *(quietly)*

The Young Pioneers are not the place for my son. He is a homosexual.

Oumansky frowns, surprised.

OUMANSKY

He is just a boy. You don't know that.

KATYA

I am his mother. And I know what will happen to him there when they find out. So do you. If you really want to help, you can make it possible for us to leave the country. Or at least just him. I have some distant cousins in France. They could take him.

Oumansky stares at her coolly.

OUMANSKY

I might think you were lying just to get an exit visa... That is a very serious crime.

> *Katya looks back at him, obviously intimidated, but holding her ground.*

> *(finally)*

I regret that you were so corrupted by your prolonged contact with western ideology. I suppose it was inevitable that any son of the amoral journalist Duranty would be poisoned from conception.

> *He returns to his pile of documents, ignoring her. She hurries out.*

LIGHTS OUT.

CURTAIN FALLS.

THE END

The Party Line intermingles historical and fictional characters.

Walter Duranty – the Pulitzer Prize-winning Moscow correspondent for The New York Times during the twenties and thirties – was very much real, as was his Russian "wife" Katya. The couple did have a son, Michael, whose life story and whereabouts are unknown.

Other historical characters in the play are Dutch politician Pim Fortuyn, Soviet press commissar Konstantin Oumansky, British occultist Aleister Crowley and movie mogul Cecil B. DeMille.

The character of Sid Brody was suggested by the life of journalist Eugene Lyons who wrote several books on the Soviet Union.

Other characters are fictional composites.

ABOUT THE AUTHORS

ROGER L. SIMON *is the author of eleven books, among them the award-winning Moses Wine detective series and a memoir,* Turning Right at Hollywood & Vine. *He is also the screenwriter of seven feature films, including* Enemies, A Love Story *and* A Better Life, *both Academy Award nominated. He is currently C E O of P J Media.*

SHERYL LONGIN *is a screenwriter and author. Among her credits are the films,* Dick *and* Prague Duet, *and a novel,* Dorian Greyhound: A Dog's Tale. The Party Line *is her first play.*

RONALD RADOSH *is Prof. Emeritus of History at the City University of New York, a columnist for PJ Media, and an Adjunct Fellow at the Hudson Institute. He is author or co-author of more than fifteen books, including* The Rosenberg File *and* A Safe Haven: Harry S. Truman and the Founding of Israel. *He is currently writing, with Allis Radosh, a book on the presidency of Warren G. Harding.*

A Note on the Type

The Party Line has been set in Kingfisher, a family of types designed by Jeremy Tankard. Frustrated by the paucity of truly well-drawn fonts for book work, Tankard set out to create a series of types that would be suitable for a wide range of text settings. Informed by a number of elegant historical precedents – the highly regarded Doves type, Monotype Barbou, and Ehrhardt among them – yet beholden to no one type in particular, Kingfisher attains a balance of formality, detail, and color that is sometimes lacking in types derived or hybridized from historical forms. The italic, designed intentionally as a complement to the roman, has much in common with earlier explorations in sloped romans like the Perpetua and Joanna italics, yet moderates the awkward elements that mar types like Van Krimpen's Romulus italic. The resulting types, modern, crisp, and handsome, are ideal for the composition of text matter at a variety of sizes, and comfortable for extended reading.

SERIES DESIGN BY CARL W. SCARBROUGH